HISTORIC GIRLS

HISTORIC GIRLS
by E. S. Brooks

Twelve stories are offered here of real girls who influenced histori-
cal events through courage, perserverance and fortitude. Learn
about Zenobia of Palmyra, Helena of Britain, Pulcheria of
Constantinople, Clotilda of Burgundy, Woo of Whang-Ho, Edith
of Scotland, Jacqueline of Holland (featured on our cover),
Catarina of Venice, Theresa of Avila, Elizabeth of Tudor, Christina
of Sweden, and Ma-Ta-Oka of Pow-Ha-Tan (or Pocahontas). This
volume is also an excellent introduction to the study of history.
Originally compiled in 1887 from selections which first appeared
in Saint Nicholas magazine, they will delight today's young girls as
much as they did their great-grandmothers when these tales first
were written.

Elbridge Streeter Brooks was born in Lowell, Massachusetts, April
14, 1846 and died in Somerville on January 7, 1902. He wrote
many books and stories for children including Historic Boys
(1885), Chilvalric Days (1886), and The Story of New York (1888).

Paperback: 0-918736-07-2 $14.95
Hardback: 0-918736-06-4 $26.95

Published by Castle Keep Press

Address inquiries to:

James A. Rock & Company, Publishers
9710 Traville Gateway Drive, Box 305
Rockville, MD 20850

E-mail: jrock@rockpublishing.com
Internet URL: www.rockpublishing.com

"'T IS A FALSE AND LYING CHARGE"

HISTORIC GIRLS

STORIES OF GIRLS WHO HAVE INFLUENCED
THE HISTORY OF THEIR TIMES

by

E. S. BROOKS

AUTHOR OF "CHIVALRIC DAYS," "HISTORIC BOYS," ETC.

CASTLE KEEP PRESS

CLASSICS REVISITED

2000

Historic Girls, by E. S. Brooks was originally published in 1887.
This volume was reproduced in facsimile from the 1908 printing,
issued in G. P. Putnam's popular Knickerbocker Series.

CASTLE KEEP PRESS
is an imprint of JAMES A. ROCK & CO., PUBLISHERS

Address comments and inquiries to:

James A. Rock & Company, Publishers
113 N. Washington Street, Box 347
Rockville, MD 20850

E-mail: jrock@rockpublishing.com
Internet URL: www.rockpublishing.com

Paperbound, ISBN: 0-918736-07-2
Hardbound, ISBN: 0-918736-06-4

Printed in the United States of America.

First Castle Keep Press Edition: August 2000

The CASTLE KEEP PRESS *Classics Revisited* series presents a selection
of hitherto hard-to-find classic works from a variety of
fields, chosen for their enduring quality and their
ability to enrich the lives of today's readers.

PREFACE.

IN these progressive days, when so much energy and discussion are devoted to what is termed equality and the rights of woman, it is well to remember that there have been in the distant past women, and girls even, who by their actions and endeavors proved themselves the equals of the men of their time in valor, shrewdness, and ability

This volume seeks to tell for the girls and boys of to-day the stories of some of their sisters of the long-ago,—girls who by eminent position or valiant deeds became historic even before they had passed the charming season of girlhood.

Their stories are fruitful of varying lessons, for some of these historic girls were wilful as well as courageous, and mischievous as well as tender-hearted.

But from all the lessons and from all the morals, one truth stands out most clearly—the fact that age and country, time and surroundings, make but little change in the real girl-nature, that has ever been impulsive, trusting, tender, and true, alike in the days of the Syrian Zenobia and in those of the modern American school-girl.

After all, whatever the opportunity, whatever the limitation, whatever the possibilities of this same never-changing girl-nature, no better precept can be laid down for our own bright young maidens, as none better can be deduced from the stories herewith presented, than that phrased in Kingsley's noble yet simple verse :

> " Be good, sweet maid, and let who will be clever ;
>   Do noble things, not dream them, all day long ;
> And so make life, death, and the vast forever
>   One grand, sweet song."

Grateful acknowledgment is made by the author for the numerous expressions of interest that came to him from his girl-readers as the papers now gathered into book-form appeared from time to time in the pages of *St. Nicholas.* The approval of those for whom one studies and labors is the pleasantest and most enduring return.

CONTENTS.

LIST OF ILLUSTRATIONS.

Due credit should be given to The Century Co. and the D. Lothrop Co. for the use of important cuts, and to the editors of *St. Nicholas* for courtesy in the privilege of an early use of the final papers.

ZENOBIA OF PALMYRA

THE GIRL OF THE SYRIAN DESERT,

[Afterward known as " Zenobia Augusta, Queen of the East."]
A.D. 250.

MANY and many miles and many days' journey toward the rising sun, over seas and mountains and deserts,—farther to the east than Rome, or Constantinople, or even Jerusalem and old Damascus,—stand the ruins of a once mighty city, scattered over a mountain-walled oasis of the great Syrian desert, thirteen hundred feet above the sea, and just across the northern border of Arabia. Look for it in your geographies. It is known as Palmyra. To-day the jackal prowls through its deserted streets and the lizard suns himself on its fallen columns, while thirty or forty miserable Arabian huts huddle together in a small corner of what was once the great court-yard of the magnificent Temple of the Sun.

And yet, sixteen centuries ago, Palmyra, or Tad-

mor as it was originally called, was one of the most
beautiful cities in the world.   Nature and art combined to make it glorious.   Like a glittering mirage
out of the sand-swept desert arose its palaces and
temples and grandly sculptured archways.   With
aqueducts and monuments and gleaming porticos ;
with countless groves of palm-trees and gardens full
of verdure; with wells and fountains, market and
circus ; with broad streets stretching away to the
city gates and lined on either side with magnificent
colonnades of rose-colored marble—such was Palmyra in the year of our Lord 250, when, in the soft
Syrian month of Nisan, or April, in an open portico
in the great colonnade and screened from the sun
by gayly colored awnings, two young people—a
boy of sixteen and a girl of twelve—looked down
upon the beautiful Street of the Thousand Columns, as lined with bazaars and thronged with
merchants it stretched from the wonderful Temple
of the Sun to the triple Gate-way of the Sepulchre,
nearly a mile away.

Both were handsome and healthy—true children
of old Tadmor, that glittering, fairy-like city which,
Arabian legends say, was built by the genii for the
great King Solomon ages and ages ago.   Midway
between the Mediterranean and the Euphrates,
it was the meeting-place for the caravans from the
east and the wagon trains from the west, and it had

RUINS OF PALMYRA.

thus become a city of merchant princes, a wealthy
commercial republic, like Florence and Venice in
the middle ages—the common toll-gate for both
the East and West.

But, though a tributary colony of Rome, it was
so remote a dependency of that mighty mistress of
the world that the yoke of vassalage was but carelessly worn and lightly felt.   The great merchants
and chiefs of caravans who composed its senate and
directed its affairs, and whose glittering statues lined
the sculptured cornice of its marble colonnades, had
more power and influence than the far-off Emperor
at Rome, and but small heed was paid to the slender garrison that acted as guard of honor to the
strategi or special officers who held the colony for
Rome and received its yearly tribute.   And yet so
strong a force was Rome in the world that even this
free - tempered desert city had gradually become
Romanized in manners as in name, so that Tadmor
had become first Adrianapolis and then Palmyra.
And this influence had touched even these children
in the portico.   For their common ancestor — a
wealthy merchant of a century before—had secured
honor and rank from the Emperor Septimus Severus
—the man who " walled in " England, and of whom
it was said that " he never performed an act of
humanity or forgave a fault."   Becoming, by the
Emperor's grace, a Roman citizen, this merchant of

Palmyra, according to a custom of the time, took the name of his royal patron as that of his own "*fahdh*," or family, and the father of young Odhainat in the portico, as was Odhainat himself, was known as Septimus Odænathus, while the young girl found her Arabic name of Bath Zabbai, Latinized into that of Septima Zenobia.

But as, thinking nothing of all this, they looked lazily on the throng below, a sudden exclamation from the lad caused his companion to raise her flashing black eyes inquiringly to his face.

" What troubles you, my Odhainat ? " she asked.

" There, there ; look there, Bath Zabbai ! " replied the boy excitedly ; " coming through the Damascus arch, and we thought him to be in Emesa."

The girl's glance followed his guiding finger, but even as she looked a clear trumpet peal rose above the din of the city, while from beneath a sculptured archway that spanned a colonnaded cross-street the bright April sun gleamed down upon the standard of Rome with its eagle crest and its S. P. Q. R. design beneath. There is a second trumpet peal, and swinging into the great Street of the Thousand Columns, at the head of his light-armed legionaries, rides the centurion Rufinus, lately advanced to the rank of tribune of one of the chief Roman cohorts in Syria. His coming, as Odhainat and even the

young Bath Zabbai knew, meant a stricter supervision of the city, a re-enforcement of its garrison,
and the assertion of the mastership of Rome over
this far eastern province on the Persian frontier.

"But why should the coming of the Roman so
trouble you, my Odhainat?" she asked. "We
are neither Jew nor Christian that we should fear
his wrath, but free Palmyreans who bend the knee
neither to Roman nor Persian masters."

"Who *will* bend the knee no longer, be it never
so little, my cousin," exclaimed the lad hotly, "as
this very day would have shown had not this crafty
Rufinus—may great Solomon's genii dash him in
the sea!—come with his cohort to mar our measures! Yet see—who cometh now?" he cried;
and at once the attention of the young people was
turned in the opposite direction as they saw, streaming out of the great fortress-like court-yard of the
Temple of the Sun, another hurrying throng.

Then young Odhainat gave a cry of joy.

"See, Bath Zabbai; they come, they come"!
he cried. "It is my father, Odhainat the *esarkos*,*
with all the leaders and all the bowmen and spearmen of our *fahdh* armed and in readiness. This
day will we fling off the Roman yoke and become
the true and unconquered lords of Palmyra. And
I, too, must join them," he added.

* The " head man," or chief of the "*fahdh*," or family.

But the young girl detained him. "Wait, cousin," she said; "watch and wait. Our *fahdh* will scarce attempt so brave a deed to-day, with these new Roman soldiers in our gates. That were scarcely wise."

But the boy broke out again. "So; they have seen each other," he said; "both sides are pressing on!"

"True; and they will meet under this very por tico," said Bath Zabbai, and moved both by interest and desire this dark-eyed Syrian girl, to whom fear was never known, standing by her cousin's side, looked down upon the tossing sea of spears and lances and glittering shields and helmets that swayed and surged in the street below.

"So, Odænathus!" said Rufinus, the tribune, reining in his horse and speaking in harsh and commanding tones, "what meaneth this array of armed followers?"

"Are the movements of Septimus Odænathus, the head-man, of such importance to the noble tribune that he must needs question a free merchant of Palmyra as to the number and manner of his servants?" asked Odænathus haughtily.

"Dog of a Palmyrean; slave of a camel-driver!" said the Roman angrily, "trifle not with me. Were you ten times the free merchant you claim, you should not thus reply. Free, forsooth! None are free but Romans."

"Have a care, O Rufinus," said the Palmyrean boldly, "choose wiser words if you would have peaceful ways. Palmyra brooks no such slander of her foremost men."

"And Rome brooks no such men as you, traitor," said Rufinus. "Ay, traitor, I say!" he repeated, as Odænathus started at the word. "Think not to hide your plots to overthrow the Roman power in your city and hand the rule to the base Sapor of Persia. Every thing is known to our great father the Emperor, and thus doth he reckon with traitors. Macrinus, strike!" and at his word the short Gallic sword in the ready hand of the big German foot-soldier went straight to its mark and Odænathus, the "head-man" of Palmyra, lay dead in the Street of the Thousand Columns.

So sudden and so unexpected was the blow that the Palmyreans stood as if stunned, unable to comprehend what had happened. But the Roman was swift to act.

"Sound, trumpets! Down, pikes!" he cried, and as the trumpet peal rose loud and clear, fresh legionaries came hurrying through the Damascus arch, and the *pilum* * and *spatha* of Rome bore back the shields and lances of Palmyra.

But, before the lowered pikes could fully disperse

---

* The *pilum* was the Roman pike, and the *spatha* the short single-edged Roman sword.

the crowd, the throng parted and through the swaying mob there burst a lithe and flying figure—a
brown-skinned maid of twelve with streaming hair,
loose robe, and angry, flashing eyes. Right under
the lowered pikes she darted and, all flushed and
panting, defiantly faced the astonished Rufinus.
Close behind her came an equally excited lad who,
when he saw the stricken body of his father on the
marble street, flung himself weeping upon it. But
Bath Zabbai's eyes flashed still more angrily :

"Assassin, murderer !" she cried ; "you have
slain my kinsman and Odhainat's father. How
dare you ; how dare you !" she repeated vehe-
mently, and then, flushing with deeper scorn, she
added : "Roman, I hate you ! Would that I were a
man. Then should all Palmyra know how——"

"Scourge these children home," broke in the
stern Rufinus, "or fetch them by the ears to their
nurses and their toys. Let the boys and girls of
Palmyra beware how they mingle in the matters of
their elders, or in the plots of their fathers. Men
of Palmyra, you who to-day have dared to think of
rebellion, look on your leader here and know how
Rome deals with traitors. But, because the merchant Odænathus bore a Roman name, and was of
Roman rank—ho, soldiers ! bear him to his house,
and let Palmyra pay such honor as befits his name
and station."

The struggling children were half led, half carried into the sculptured *atrium* * of the palace of Odæ- nathus which, embowered in palms and vines and wonderful Eastern plants, stood back from the mar- ble colonnade on the Street of the Thousand Col- umns. And when in that same *atrium* the body of the dead merchant lay embalmed and draped for its " long home," † there, kneeling by the stricken form of the murdered father and kinsman, and with up- lifted hand, after the vindictive manner of these fierce old days of blood, Odænathus and Zenobia swore eternal hatred to Rome.

Hatred, boys and girls, is a very ugly as it is a very headstrong fault ; but as there is a good side even to a bad habit, so there is a hatred which may rise to the heighth of a virtue. Hatred of vice *is* virtue ; hatred of tyranny is patriotism. It is this which has led the world from slavery to freedom, from ignorance to enlightenment, and inspired the words that have found immortality alike above the ashes of Bradshaw the regicide and of Jefferson the American : " Rebellion to tyrants is obedience to God."

But how could a fatherless boy and girl, away off

* The large central " living-room " of a Roman palace.

† The Palmyreans built great tower-tombs, beautiful in architecture and adornment, the ruins of which still stand on the hill slopes overlooking the old city. These they called their " long homes," and you will find the word used in the same sense in Ecclesiastes xii., 5.

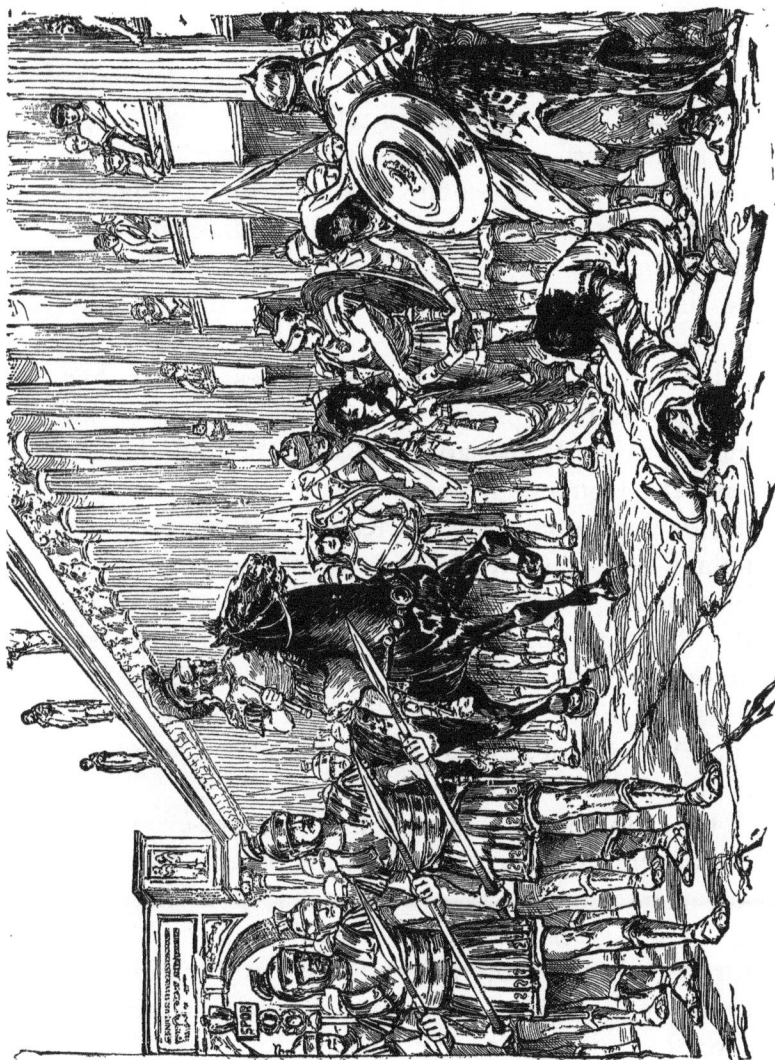

ZENOBIA'S DEFIANCE OF THE ROMAN TRIBUNE IN THE STREET OF THE THOUSAND COLUMNS.

on the edge of an Arabian desert, hope to resist successfully the mighty power of Imperial Rome? The story of their lives will tell.

If there are some people who are patriots, there are others who are poltroons, and such a one was Hairan, the elder brother of young Odhainat, when, succeeding to his dead father's wealth and power, he thought less of Roman tyranny than of Roman gold.

"Revenge ourselves on their purses, my brother, and not on their pikes," he said. "'T is easier and more profitable to sap the Roman's gold than to shed the Roman's blood."

But this submission to Rome only angered Odhainat, and to such a conflict of opinion did it lead that at last Hairan drove his younger brother from the home of his fathers, and the lad, "an Esau among the Jacobs of Tadmor," so the record tells us, spent his youth amid the roving Bedaween of the Arabian deserts and the mountaineers of the Armenian hills, waiting his time.

But, though a homeless exile, the dark-eyed Bath Zabbai did not forget him. In the palace of another kinsman, Septimus Worod, the "lord of the markets," she gave herself up to careful study, and hoped for the day of Palmyra's freedom. As rich in powers of mind as in the graces of form and face, she soon became a wonderful scholar for those distant days—mistress of four languages : Coptic, Syriac, Latin, and Greek, while the fiery temper of the girl grew into the nobler ambitions of the maiden. But above all things, as became her mingled Arabic and Egyptian blood—for she could trace her ancestry back to the free chiefs of the Arabian desert, and to the dauntless Cleopatra of Egypt,—she loved the excitement of the chase, and in the plains and mountains beyond the city she learned to ride and hunt with all the skill and daring of a young Diana.

And so it came to pass that when the Emperor Valerian sent an embassy from Rome to Ctesiphon, bearing a message to the Great King, as Sapor, the Persian monarch, was called, the embassy halted in Palmyra, and Septimus Hairan, now the head-man of the city, ordered, "in the name of the senate and people of Palmyra," a grand *venatio*, or wild beast hunt, in the circus near the Street of the Thousand Columns, in honor of his Roman guests. And he despatched his kinsman Septimus Zabbai, the soldier, to the Armenian hills to superintend the capture and delivery of the wild game needed for the hunt. With a great following of slaves and huntsmen, Zabbai the soldier departed, and with him went his niece, Bath Zabbai, or Zenobia, now a fearless young huntress of fifteen. Space will not permit to tell of the wonders and excitement of that wild-beast hunt—a hunt in which none must be

killed but all must be captured without mar or
wound.   Such a trapping of wolves and bears and
buffaloes was there, such a setting of nets and pit-
falls for the mountain lion and the Syrian leopard,
while the Arab hunters beat, and drove, and shouted,
or lay in wait with net and blunted lance, that it was
rare sport to the fearless Zenobia, who rode her
fleet Arabian horse at the very head of the chase,
and, with quick eye and practised hand, helped
largely to swell the trophies of the hunt.   What
girl of to-day, whom even the pretty little jumping-
mouse of Syria would scare out of her wits, could
be tempted to witness such a scene?   And yet this
young Palmyrean girl loved nothing better than the
chase, and the records tell us that she was a "pas-
sionate hunter," and that "she pursued with ardor
the wild beasts of the desert" and thought nothing
of fatigue or peril.

So, through dense Armenian forests and along
rugged mountain paths, down rock-strewn hill-slopes
and in green, low-lying valleys, the chase swept on:
and one day, in one of the pleasant glades which,
half-sun and half-shadow, stretch away to the Leba-
non hills, young Bath Zabbai suddenly reined in her
horse in full view of one of the typical hunting
scenes of those old days.   A young Arabian hunter
had enticed a big mountain lion into one of the
strong-meshed nets of stout palm fibres, then used

for such purposes. His trained leopard or *cheetah* had drawn the beast from his lair, and by cunning devices had led him on until the unfortunate lion was half-entrapped. Just then, with a sudden swoop, a great golden eagle dashed down upon the pre-occupied *cheetah*, and buried his talons in the leopard's head. But the weight of his victim was more than he had bargained for; the *cheetah* with a quick upward dash dislodged one of the great bird's talons, and, turning as quickly, caught the disengaged leg in his sharp teeth. At that instant the lion, springing at the struggling pair, started the fastenings of the net, which, falling upon the group, held all three prisoners. The eagle and the lion thus ensnared sought to release themselves, but only ensnared themselves the more, while the cunning *cheetah*, versed in the knowledge of the hunter's net, crept out from beneath the meshes as his master raised them slightly, and with bleeding head crawled to him for praise and relief.

Then the girl, flushed with delight at this double capture, galloped to the spot, and in that instant she recognized in the successful hunter her cousin the exile.

"Well snared, my Odhainat," she said, as, the first exclamation of surprise over, she stood beside the brown-faced and sturdy young hunter. "The Palmyrean leopard hath bravely trapped both the

Roman eagle and the Persian lion. See, is it not
an omen from the gods? Face valor with valor
and craft with craft, O Odhainat ! Have you forgotten the vow in your father's palace full three
years ago?"

Forgotten it ? Not he. And then he told Bath
Zabbai how in all his wanderings he had kept their
vow in mind, and with that, too, her other words of
counsel, " Watch and Wait." He told her that, far
and wide, he was known to all the Arabs of the desert and the Armenians of the hills, and how, from
sheikh to camel-boy, the tribes were ready to join
with Palmyra against both Rome and Persia.

"Your time will indeed come, my Odhainat,"
said the fearless girl, with proud looks and ringing
voice. " See, even thus our omen gives the proof,"
and she pointed to the net, beneath whose meshes
both eagle and lion, fluttering and panting, lay
wearied with their struggles, while the *cheetah* kept
watch above them. " Now make your peace with
Hairan, your brother ; return to Palmyra once again,
and still let us watch and wait."

Three more years passed. Valerian, Emperor of
Rome, leading his legions to war with Sapor, whom
men called the " Great King," had fallen a victim
to the treachery and traps of the Persian monarch,
and was held a miserable prisoner in the Persian

capital, where, richly robed in the purple of the Roman emperors and loaded with chains, he was used by the savage Persian tyrant as a living horse-block for the sport of an equally savage court. In Palmyra, Hairan was dead, and young Odhainat, his brother, was now Septimus Odænathus—"head-man" of the city and to all appearances the firm friend of Rome.

There were great rejoicings in Palmyra when the wise Zenobia—still scarce more than a girl—and the fearless young "head-man" of the desert republic were married in the marble city of the palm-trees, and her shrewd counsels brought still greater triumphs to Odænathus and to Palmyra,

In the great market-place or forum, Odænathus and Zenobia awaited the return of their messengers to Sapor. For the "Great King," having killed and stuffed the captive Roman Emperor, now turned his arms against the Roman power in the east and, destroying both Antioch and Emesa, looked with an evil eye toward Palmyra. Zenobia, remembering the omen of the eagle and the lion, repeated her counsel of facing craft with craft, and letters and gifts had been sent to Sapor, asking for peace and friendship. There is a hurried entrance through the eastern gate of the city, and the messengers from the Palmyrean senate rush into the market-place.

"Your presents to the Great King have been thrown into the river, O Odænathus," they reported, "and thus sayeth Sapor of Persia: 'Who is this Odænathus, that he should thus presume to write to his lord? If he would obtain mitigation of the punishment that awaits him, let him fall prostrate before the foot of our throne, with his hands bound behind his back. Unless he doeth this, he, his family, and his country shall surely perish!'"

Swift to wrath and swifter still to act, Zenobia sprang to her feet. "Face force with force, Odænathus. Be strong and sure, and Palmyra shall yet humble the Persian!"

Her advice was taken. Quickly collecting the troops of Palmyra and the Arabs and Armenians who were his allies, the fearless "head-man" fell upon the army of the haughty Persian king, defeated and despoiled it, and drove it back to Persia. As Gibbon, the historian says: "The majesty of Rome, oppressed by a Persian, was protected by an Arab of Palmyra."

For this he was covered with favors by Rome; made supreme commander in the East, and, with Zenobia as his adviser and helper, each year made Palmyra stronger and more powerful.

Here, rightly, the story of the girl Zenobia ends. A woman now, her life fills one of the most bril-

liant pages of history. While her husband conquered for Rome in the north, she, in his absence,
governed so wisely in the south as to insure the
praise of all. And when the time was ripe, and
Rome, ruled by weak emperors and harassed by
wild barbarians, was in dire stress, the childish
vow of the boy and girl made years before found
fulfilment. Palmyra was suddenly declared free
from the dominion of Rome, and Odænathus was
acknowledged by senate and people as " Emperor
and King of kings."

But the hand of an assassin struck down the son
as it had stricken the father. Zenobia, ascending
the throne of Palmyra, declared herself " Zenobia
Augusta, the Empress of the East," and, after the
manner of her time, extended her empire in every
direction until, as the record says : " A small terri-
tory in the desert, under the government of a
woman, extended its conquests over many rich
countries and several states. Zenobia, lately con-
fined to the barren plains about Palmyra, now held
sway from Egypt in the south, to the Bosphorus
and the Black Sea in the north."

But a new emperor ruled in Rome: Aurelian,
soldier and statesman. " Rome," he said, "shall
never lose a province." And then the struggle for
dominion in the East began. The strength and
power of Rome, directed by the Emperor himself,

at last triumphed.   Palmyra fell, and Zenobia,
after a most heroic defence of her kingdom, was
led a prisoner to Rome.   Clad in magnificent
robes, loaded with jewels and with heavy chains of
gold, she walked, regal and undaunted still, in the
great triumphal procession of her conqueror, and,
disdaining to kill herself as did Cleopatra and
Dido, she gave herself up to the nobler work of
the education and culture of her children, and led
for many years, in her villa at Tibur, the life of a
noble Roman matron.

Such, in brief, is the story of Zenobia.   You
must read for yourselves the record of her later
years, as it stands in history, if you would know
more of her grandeur in her days of power, and her
moral grandeur in her days of defeat.

And with Zenobia ·fell Palmyra.   Centuries of
ruin and neglect have passed over the once fairy-
like city of the Syrian oasis.   Her temples and
colonnades, her monuments and archways and
wonderful buildings are prostrate and decayed, and
the site even of the glorious city has been known
to the modern world only within the last century.
But while time lasts and the record of heroic deeds
survives, neither fallen column nor ruined arch nor
all the destruction and neglect of modern barbarism can blot out the story of the life and worth of

Bath Zabbai, the brave girl of the Syrian desert, whom all the world honors as the noblest woman of antiquity—Zenobia of Palmyra, the dauntless "Queen of the East."

HELENA OF BRITAIN

THE GIRL OF THE ESSEX FELLS.

[Afterward known as " St. Helena," the mother of Constantine.]
A.D. 255.

EVER since that far-off day in the infancy of the world, when lands began to form and rivers to flow seaward, the little river Colne has wound its crooked way through the fertile fields of Essex eastward to the broad North Sea.

Through hill-land and through moor-land, past Moyns and Great Yeldham, past Halstead and Chappel and the walls of Colchester, turning now this way and now that until it comes to Mersea Island and the sea, the little river flows to-day even as it sped along one pleasant summer morning sixteen hundred and forty years ago, when a little British princess, only fairly in her teens, reclined in comfortable contentment in her gilded barge and floated down the river from her father's palace at Colchester to the strand at Wivanloe.

For this little girl of fourteen, Helena, the princess, was a king's daughter, and, according to all accounts, a very bright and charming girl besides— which all princesses have not been. Her father was Coel, second prince of Britain and king of that part of ancient England, which includes the present shires of Essex and of Suffolk, about the river Colne.

Not a very large kingdom this, but even as small as it was, King Coel did not hold it in undisputed sway. For he was one of the tributary princes of Britain, in the days when Roman arms, and Roman law, and Roman dress, and Roman manners, had place and power throughout England, from the Isle of Wight, to the Northern highlands, behind whose forest-crowned hills those savage natives known as the Picts—" the tattooed folk "—held possession of ancient Scotland, and defied the eagles of Rome.

The monotonous song of the rowers, keeping time with each dip of the broad-bladed oars, rose and fell in answer to the beats of the master's silver baton, and Helena too followed the measure with the tap, tap, of her sandaled foot.

Suddenly there shot out around one of the frequent turns in the river, the gleam of other oars, the high prow of a larger galley, and across the water came the oar-song of a larger company of rowers. Helena started to her feet.

"Look, Cleon," she cried, pointing eagerly towards the approaching boat, "'t is my father's own trireme. Why this haste to return, think'st thou?"

"I cannot tell, little mistress," replied the freedman Cleon, her galley-master; "the king thy father must have urgent tidings, to make him return thus quickly to Camalodunum."

Both the girl and the galley-master spoke in Latin, for the language of the Empire was the language of those in authority or in official life even in its remotest provinces, and the galley-master did but use the name which the Roman lords of Britain had given to the prosperous city on the Colne, in which the native prince, King Coel, had his court—the city which to-day is known under its later Saxon name of Colchester.

It was, indeed, a curious state of affairs in England. I doubt if many of my girl and boy readers, no matter how well they may stand in their history classes, have ever thought of the England of Hereward and Ivanhoe, of Paul Dombey and Tom Brown, as a Roman land.

And yet at the time when this little Flavia Julia Helena was sailing down the river Colne, the island of Britain, in its southern section at least, was almost as Roman in manner, custom, and speech as was Rome itself.

For nearly five hundred years, from the days of Cæsar the conqueror, to those of Honorius the unfortunate, was England, or Britain as it was called, a Roman province, broken only in its allegiance by the early revolts of the conquered people or by the later usurpations of ambitious and unpincipled governors.

And, at the date of our story, in the year 255 A.D., the beautiful island had so far grown out of the barbarisms of ancient Britain as to have long since forgotten the gloomy rites and open-air altars of the Druids, and all the half-savage surroundings of those stern old priests.

Everywhere Roman temples testified to the acceptance by the people of the gods of Rome, and little Helena herself each morning hung the altar of the emperor-god Claudius with garlands in the stately temple which had been built in his honor in her father's palace town, asked the protection of Cybele, "the Heavenly Virgin," and performed the rites that the Empire demanded for "the thousand gods of Rome."

Throughout the land, south of the massive wall which the great Emperor Hadrian had stretched across the island from the mouth of the Solway to the mouth of the Tyne, the people themselves who had gathered into or about the thirty growing Roman cities which the conquerors had founded

and beautified, had become Roman in language, religion, dress, and ways, while the educational influ-
ences of Rome, always following the course of her
conquering eagles, had planted schools and colleges
throughout the land, and laid the foundation for
that native learning which in later years was to
make the English nation so great and powerful.

And what a mighty empire must have been that
of Rome that, in those far-off days, when rapid
transit was unknown, and steam and electricity
both lay dormant, could have entered into the lives
of two bright young maidens so many leagues removed from one another—Zenobia, the dusky Palmyrean of the East, and Helena, the fresh-faced
English girl of the West.

But to such distant and widely separated confines
had this power of the vast Empire extended; and
to this thoughtful young princess, drifting down
the winding English river, the sense of Roman
supremacy and power would come again and again.

For this charming young girl—said, later, to
have been the most beautiful woman of her time in
England — though reared to Roman ways and
Roman speech, had too well furnished a mind not
to think for herself. "She spake," so says the
record, "many tongues and was replete with piety."
The only child of King Coel, her doting old father
had given her the finest education that Rome could

offer. She was, even before she grew to womanhood, so we are told, a fine musician, a marvellous
worker in tapestry, in hammered brass and pottery,
and was altogether as wise and wonderful a young
woman as even these later centuries can show.

But, for all this grand education, she loved to
hear the legends and stories of her people that in
various ways would come to her ears, either as the
simple tales of her British nurse, or in the wild
songs of the wandering bards, or singers.

As she listened to these she thought less of those
crude and barbaric ways of her ancestors that Rome
had so vastly bettered than of their national independence and freedom from the galling yoke of
Rome, and, as was natural, she cherished the memory of Boadicea, the warrior queen, and made a
hero of the fiery young Caractacus.

It is always so, you know. Every bright young
imagination is apt to find greater glories in the
misty past, or grander possibilities in a still more
misty future than in the too practical and prosaic
present in which both duty and destiny lie. And
so Helena the princess, leaning against the soft
cushions of her gilded barge, had sighed for the
days of the old-time British valor and freedom, and,
even as she looked off toward the approaching
triareme, she was wondering how she could awake
to thoughts of British glory her rather heavy-witted

father, Coel the King—an hereditary prince of that
ancient Britain in which he was now, alas, but a
tributary prince of the all too powerful Rome.

Now, "old King Cole," as Mother Goose tells
us—for young Helena's father was none other
than the veritable "old King Cole" of our nursery
jingle—was a "jolly old soul," and a jolly old soul
is very rarely an independent or ambitious one. So
long as he could have "his pipe and his bowl"—
not, of course, his long pipe of tobacco that all the
Mother Goose artists insist upon giving him—but
the reed pipe upon which his musicians played—so
long, in other words, as he could live in ease and
comfort, undisturbed in his enjoyment of the good
things of life by his Roman over-lords, he cared for
no change. Rome took the responsibility and he
took things easily. But this very day, while his
daughter Helena was floating down the river to
meet him on the strand at Wivanloe, he was re-
turning from an unsuccessful boar-hunt in the
Essex woods, very much out of sorts—cross because
he had not captured the big boar he had hoped to
kill, cross because his favorite musicians had been
"confiscated" by the Roman governor or propræ-
tor at Londinium (as London was then called),
and still more cross because he had that day
received dispatches from Rome demanding a
special and unexpected tax levy, or tribute, to

meet the necessary expenses of the new Emperor Diocletian.

Something else had happened to increase his ill temper. His "jolly old soul," vexed by the numerous crosses of the day, was thrown into still greater perplexity by the arrival, just as he stood fretful and chafing on the shore at Wivanloe, of one who even now was with him on the trireme, bearing him company back to his palace at Camolodunum—Carausius the admiral.

This Carausius, the admiral, was an especially vigorous, valorous, and fiery young fellow of twenty-one. He was cousin to the Princess Helena and a prince of the blood royal of ancient Britain. Educated under the strict military system of Rome, he had risen to distinction in the naval force of the Empire, and was now the commanding officer in the northern fleet that had its central station at Gessoriacum, now Boulogne, on the northern coast of France. He had chased and scattered the German pirates who had so long ravaged the northern seas, had been named by the Emperor admiral of the north, and was the especial pride, as he was the dashing young leader, of the Roman sailors along the English Channel and the German shores.

The light barge of the princess approached the heavier boat of the king, her father. At her signal the oarsmen drew up alongside, and, scarce waiting for either boat to more than slacken speed, the nimble-footed girl sprang lightly to the deck of her father's galley. Then bidding the obedient Cleon take her own barge back to the palace, she hurried at once, and without question, like the petted only child she was, into the high-raised cabin at the stern, where beneath the Roman standards sat her father the king.

Helena entered the apartment at a most exciting moment. For there, facing her portly old father, whose clouded face bespoke his troubled mind, stood her trimly-built young cousin Carausius the admiral, bronzed with his long exposure to the sea-blasts, a handsome young viking, and, in the eyes of the hero-loving Helen, very much of a hero because of his acknowledged daring and his valorous deeds.

Neither man seemed to have noticed the sudden entrance of the girl, so deep were they in talk.

"I tell thee, uncle," the hot-headed admiral was saying, "it is beyond longer bearing. This new emperor—this Diocletian—who is he to dare to dictate to a prince of Britain? A foot-soldier of Illyria, the son of slaves, and the client of three coward emperors; an assassin, so it hath been said, who from chief of the domestics, hath become by his own cunning Emperor of Rome.

And now hath he dared to accuse me—me, a free Briton and a Roman citizen as well, a prince and the son of princes, with having taken bribes from these German pirates whom I have vanquished. He hath openly said that I, Carausius the admiral, have filled mine own coffers while neglecting the revenues of the state. I will not bear it. I am a better king than he, did I but have my own just rights, and even though he be Diocletian the Emperor, he needeth to think twice before he dare accuse a prince of Britain with bribe-taking and perjury."

" True enough, good nephew," said **King Coel**, as the admiral strode up and down before him, angrily playing with the hilt of his short Roman sword, " true enough, and I too have little cause to love this low-born emperor. He hath taken from me both my players and my gold, when I can illy spare either from my comfort or my necessities. 'T is a sad pass for Britain. But Rome is mistress now. What may we hope to do ?"

The Princess Helena sprang to her father's side, her young face flushed, her small hand raised in emphasis. " Do !" cried she, and the look of defiance flamed on her fair young face. " Do ! Is it thou, my father, thou, my cousin, princes of Britain both, that ask so weak a question ? O that I were a man ! What did that brave enemy of our

house, Cassivellaunus, do? what Caractacus? what
the brave queen Boadicea?   When the Roman
drove them to despair they raised the standard of
revolt, sounded their battle cries, and showed the
Roman that British freemen could fight to the
death for their country and their home.   And thus
should we do, without fear or question, and see
here again in Britain a victorious kingdom ruled
once more by British kings."

"Nay, nay, my daughter," said cautious King
Coel, "your words are those of an unthinking girl.
The power of Rome ——— "

But the Prince Carausius, as the girl's brave
words rang out, gave her an admiring glance, and,
crossing to where she stood, laid his hand approv-
ingly upon her shoulder.

"The girl is right, uncle," he said, breaking in
upon the king's cautious speech.   "Too long have
we bowed the neck to Roman tyranny.   We, free
princes of Britain that we are, have it even now in
our power to stand once again as altogether free.
The fleet is mine, the people are yours, if you will
but amuse them.   Our brothers are groaning under
the load of Roman tribute, and are ripe to strike.
Raise the cry at Camalodunum, my uncle; cry:
'Havoc and death to Rome!'   My fleet shall pour
its victorious sailors upon the coast; the legions,
even now full of British fighters, shall flock to our

united standands, and we shall rule—Emperors in the North, even as do the Roman conquerors rule Emperors in the South."

Young blood often sways and leads in council and in action, especially when older minds are over-cautious or sluggish in decision. The words of Carausius and Helena carried the day with Coel the king, already smarting under a sense of ill-treatment by his Roman over-lords.

The standard of revolt was raised in Camalodunum. The young admiral hurried back to France to make ready his fleet, while Coel the king, spurred on to action by the patriotic Helena, who saw herself another Boadicea—though, in truth, a younger and much fairer one—gathered a hasty following, won over to his cause the British-filled legion in his palace-town, and, descending upon the nearest Roman camps and stations, surprised, captured, scattered, or brought over their soldiers, and proclaimed himself free from the yoke of Rome and supreme prince of Britain.

Ambition is always selfish. Even when striving for the general good there lies, too often, beneath this noble motive the still deeper one of selfishness. Carausius the admiral, though determined upon kingly power, had no desire for a divided supremacy. He was determined to be sole emperor, or none. Crafty and unscrupulous, although brave and

high-spirited, he deemed it wisest to delay his part
of the compact until he should see how it fared
with his uncle, the king, and then, upon his defeat,
to climb to certain victory.

He therefore sent to his uncle promises instead
of men, and when summoned by the Roman governor to assist in putting down the revolt, he returned loyal answers, but sent his aid to neither
party.

King Coel after his first successes knew that,
unaided, he could not hope to withstand the Roman
force that must finally be brought against him.
Though urged to constant action by his wise young
daughter, he preferred to do nothing ; and, satisfied with the acknowledgment of his power in and
about his little kingdom on the Colne, he spent
his time in his palace with the musicians that he
loved so well, and the big bowl of liquor that he
loved, it is to be feared, quite as dearly.

The musicians—the pipers and the harpers—
sang his praises, and told of his mighty deeds, and,
no doubt, their refrain was very much the same as
the one that has been preserved for us in the jingle
of Mother Goose :

> " O, none so rare as can compare
>   With King Cole and his fiddlers three."

But if the pleasure-loving old king was list-
less, young Helena was not. The misty records

speak of her determined efforts, and though it is hard to understand how a girl of fifteen can do any thing toward successful generalship, much can be granted to a young lady who, if the records speak truth, was, even while a girl, "a Minerva in wisdom, and not deficient in statecraft."

So, while she advised with her father's boldest captains and strengthened so wisely the walls of ancient Colchester, or Camalodunum, that traces of her work still remain as proof of her untiring zeal, she still cherished the hope of British freedom and release from Rome. And the loving old king, deep in his pleasures, still recognized the will and wisdom of his valiant daughter, and bade his artists make in her honor a memorial that should ever speak of her valor. And this memorial, lately unearthed, and known as the Colchester Sphinx, perpetuates the lion-like qualities of a girl in her teens, who dared withstand the power of Imperial Rome.

And still no help came from her cousin, the admiral. But one day a galley speeding up the Colne brought this unsigned message to King Coel:

"*To Coel, King in Camalodunum, Greeting:*

'Save thyself. Constantius the sallow-faced, prefect of the Western prætorians, is even now on his way from Spain to crush thy revolt. Save thyself. I wait. Justice will come."

"Thou seest, O daughter," said King Coel as
Helena read the craven missive, "the end cometh as I knew it would.   Well, man can but die."
And with this philosophic reflection the "jolly old
soul" only dipped his red nose still deeper into his
big bowl, and bade his musicians play their loudest
and merriest.

But Helena,   "not deficient in   statecraft,"
thought for both.   She would save her father, her
country, and herself, and shame her disloyal cousin.
Discretion is the better part of valor.   Let us see
how discreet a little lady was this fair young Princess Helena.

The legions came to Camalodunum.   Across
Gaul and over the choppy channel they came,
borne by the very galleys that were to have suc-
cored the British king.   Up through the mouth of
Thames they sailed, and landing at Londinium,
marched in close array along the broad Roman
road that led straight up to the gates of Camalodunum.   Before the walls of Camalodunum was
pitched the Roman camp, and the British king was
besieged in his own palace-town.

The Roman trumpets sounded before the gate
of the beleaguered city, and the herald of the prefect, standing out from his circle of guards, cried
the summons to surrender:

"Coel of Britain, traitor to the Roman people

and to thy lord the Emperor, hear thou! In the name of the Senate and People of Rome, I, Constantius the prefect, charge thee to deliver up to them ere this day's sun shall set, this, their City of Camalodunum, and thine own rebel body as well. Which done they will in mercy pardon the crime of treason to the city, and will work their will and punishment only upon thee—the chief rebel. And if this be not done within the appointed time, then will the walls of this their town of Camalodunum be overthrown, and thou and all thy people be given the certain death of traitors."

King Coel heard the summons, and some spark of that very patriotism that had inspired and incited his valiant little daughter flamed in his heart. He would have returned an answer of defiance. " I can at least die with my people," he said, but young Helena interposed.

" Leave this to me, my father," she said. " As I have been the cause, so let me be the end of trouble. Say to the prefect that in three hours' time the British envoy will come to his camp with the king's answer to his summons."

The old king would have replied otherwise, but his daughter's entreaties and the counsels of his captains who knew the hopelessness of resistance, forced him to assent, and his herald made answer accordingly.

Constantius the prefect—a manly, pleasant-
looking young commander, called *Chlorus* or "the
sallow," from his pale face,—sat in his tent within
the Roman camp.   The three hours' grace allowed
had scarcely expired when his sentry announced
the arrival of the envoy of Coel of Britain.

" Bid him enter," said the prefect.   Then, as the
curtains of his tent were drawn aside, the prefect
started in surprise, for there before him stood, not
the rugged form of a British fighting man, but
a fair young girl, who bent her graceful head in
reverent obeisance to the youthful representative
of the Imperial Cæsars.

"What would'st thou with me, maiden ?" asked
the prefect.

" I am the daughter of Coel of Britain," said the
girl, "and I am come to sue for pardon and for
peace."

" The Roman people have no quarrel with the
girls of Britain," said the prefect.   "Hath then
King Coel fallen so low in state that a maiden
must plead for him ?"

" He hath not fallen at all, O Prefect," replied
the girl proudly ; "the king, my father, would
withstand thy force but that I, his daughter, know
the cause of this unequal strife, and seek to make
terms with the victors."

The girl's fearlessness pleased the prefect, for

Constantius Chlorus was a humane and gentle man, fierce enough in fight, but seeking never to needlessly wound an enemy or lose a friend.

"And what are thy terms, fair envoy of Britain?" he demanded.

"These, O Prefect," replied Helena, "If but thou wilt remove thy cohorts to Londinium, I pledge my father's faith and mine, that he will, within five days, deliver to thee as hostage for his fealty, myself and twenty children of his councillors and captains. And further, I, Helena the princess, will bind myself to deliver up to thee, with the hostages, the chief rebel in this revolt, and the one to whose counselling this strife with Rome is due."

Both the matter and the manner of the offered terms still further pleased the prefect, and he said: "Be it so, Princess." Then summoning his lieutenant, he said: "Conduct the envoy of Coel of Britain with all courtesy to the gates of the the city," and with a herald's escort the girl returned to her father.

Again the old king rebelled at the terms his daughter had made.

"I know the ways of Rome," he said. "I know what their mercy meaneth. Thou shalt never go as hostage for my faith, O daughter, nor carry out this hazardous plan."

" I have pledged my word and thine, O King,"
said Helena.   " Surely a Briton's pledge should
be as binding as a Roman's."

So she carried her point, and, in five days' time,
she, with twenty of the boys and girls of Camalodunum, went as hostages to the Roman camp in
London.

" Here be thy hostages, fair Princess," said Constantius the prefect as he received the children ;
" and this is well.   But remember the rest of thy
compact.   Deliver to me now, according to thy
promise, the chief rebel against Rome."

" She is here, O Prefect, "said the intrepid girl.
" I am that rebel—Helena of Britain ! "

The smile upon the prefect's face changed to
sudden sternness.

"Trifle not with Roman justice, girl," he said,
" I demand the keeping of thy word."

" It is kept," replied the princess.   " Helena of
Britain is the cause and motive of this revolt
against Rome.   If it be rebellion for a free prince
to claim his own, if it be rebellion for a prince to
withstand for the sake of his people the unjust
demands of the conqueror, if it be rebellion for one
who loveth her father to urge that father to valiant
deeds in defence of the liberties of the land over.
which he ruleth as king, then am I a rebel, for I
have done all these, and only because of my words

"LEAVE THIS TO ME, MY FATHER," SAID HELENA.

did the king, my father, take up arms against the might and power of Rome. I am the chief rebel. Do with me as thou wilt."

And now the prefect saw that the girl spoke the truth, and that she had indeed kept her pledge.

"Thy father and his city are pardoned," he announced after a few moments of deliberation. "Remain thou here, thou and thy companions, as hostages for Britain, until such time as I shall determine upon the punishment due to one who is so fierce a rebel against the power of Rome."

So the siege of Camalodunum was raised, and the bloodless rebellion ended. Constantius the prefect took up his residence for a while within King Coel's city, and at last returned to his command in Gaul and Spain, well pleased with the spirit of the little maiden whom, so he claimed, he still held in his power as the prisoner of Rome.

Constantius the prefect came again to Britain, and with a greater following, fully ten years after King Coel's revolt, for now, again, rebellion was afoot in the island province.

Carausius the admiral, biding his time, sought at last to carry out his scheme of sole supremacy. Sailing with his entire war-fleet to Britain, he won the legions to his side, proclaimed himself Emperor of Britain, and defied the power of Rome.

So daring and successful was his move that Rome

for a time was powerless. Carausius was recognized as "associate" emperor by Rome, until such time as she should be ready to punish his rebellion, and for seven years he reigned as emperor of Britain.

But ere this came to pass, Helena the princess had gone over to Gaul, and had become the wife of Constantius the prefect,—"Since only thus," said he, "may I keep in safe custody this prisoner of Rome."

The imperial power of Carausius was but short-lived. Crafty himself, he fell a victim to the craft of others, and the sword of Allectus, his chief minister and most trusted confidant, ended his life when once again the power of Rome seemed closing about the little kingdom of Britain.

Constantius became governor of Britain, and finally cæsar and emperor. But, long before that day arrived, the Princess Helena had grown into a loyal Roman wife and mother, dearly loving her little son Constantine, who, in after years, became the first and greatest Christian emperor of Rome.

She bestowed much loving care upon her native province of Britain. She became a Christian even before her renowned son had his historic vision of the flaming cross. When more than eighty years old she made a pilgrimage to the Holy Land. There she did many good and kindly deeds, erected temples above the Sepulchre of the Saviour, at his birthplace at Bethlehem, and on the Mount of Olives. She is said, also, to have discovered upon Calvary the cross upon which had suffered and died the Saviour she had learned to worship.

Beloved throughout her long and useful life she was canonized after her death, and is now recognized one of the saints of the Romish church.

To-day in the city of London you may see the memorial church reared to her memory — the Church of Great St. Helena, in Bishopgate. A loving, noble, wonderful, and zealous woman, she is a type of the brave young girlhood of the long ago, and, however much of fiction there may be mingled with the fact of her life-story, she was, we may feel assured, all that the chroniclers have claimed for her—" one of the grandest women of the earlier centuries."

PULCHERIA OF CONSTANTINOPLE

The girl of the golden horn

[*Afterward known as "Pulcheria Augusta, Empress of the East."*]
A.D. 413.

HERE was trouble and confusion in the imperial palace of Theodosius the Little, Emperor of the East. Now, this Theodosius was called "the Little" because, though he bore the name of his mighty grandfather, Theodosius the Great, emperor of both the East and West, he had as yet done nothing worthy any other title than that of "the Little," or "the Child." For Theodosius emperor though he was called, was only a boy of twelve, and not a very bright boy at that.

His father, Arcadius the emperor, and his mother, Eudoxia the empress, were dead; and in the great palace at Constantinople, in this year of grace, 413, Theodosius, the boy emperor, and his three sisters, Pulcheria, Marina, and Arcadia, alone were left to uphold the tottering dignity and the empty name of the once mighty Empire of the East, which their great ancestors, Constantine and Theodosius, had established and strengthened.

And now there was confusion in the imperial palace; for word came in haste from the Dacian border that Ruas, king of the Huns, sweeping down from the east, was ravaging the lands along the Upper Danube, and with his host of barbarous warriors was defeating the legions and devastating the lands of the empire.

The wise Anthemius, prefect of the east, and governor or guardian of the young emperor, was greatly disturbed by the tidings of this new invasion. Already he had repelled at great cost the first advance of these terrible Huns, and had quelled into a sort of half submission the less ferocious followers of Ulpin the Thracian; but now he knew that his armies along the Danube were in no condition to withstand the hordes of Huns, that, pouring in from distant Siberia, were following the lead of Ruas, their king, for plunder and booty, and were even now encamped scarce two hundred and fifty miles from the seven gates and the triple walls of splendid Constantinople.

Turbaned Turks, mosques and minarets, muftis and cadis, veiled eastern ladies, Mohammedans and muezzins, Arabian Nights and attar of roses, bazars, dogs, and donkeys—these, I suppose, are what Constantinople suggests whenever its name is mentioned to any girl or boy of to-day,—the capital of modern Turkey, the city of the Sublime Porte. But the greatest glory of Constantinople was away back in the early days before the time of Mohammed, or of the Crusaders, when it was the centre of the Christian religion, the chief and gorgeous capital of a Christian empire, and the residence of Christian emperors,—from the days of Constantine the conqueror to those of Justinian the law-giver and of Irene the empress. It was the metropolis of the eastern half of the great Roman Empire, and during this period of over five hundred years all the wealth and treasure of the east poured into Constantinople, while all the glories of the empire, even the treasures of old Rome itself, were drawn upon to adorn and beautify this rival city by the Golden Horn. And so in the days of Theodosius the Little, the court of Constantinople, although troubled with fear of a barbarian invasion and attack, glittered with all the gorgeousness and display of the most magnificent empire in the world.

In the great *daphne*, or central space of the imperial palace, the prefect Anthemius, with the young emperor, the three princesses, and their gorgeously arrayed nobles and attendants, awaited, one day, the envoys of Ruas the Hun, who sought lands and power within the limits of the empire.

They came, at last,—great, fierce-looking fellows, not at all pleasant to contemplate—big-boned, broad-shouldered, flat-nosed, swarthy, and small-eyed, with war-cloaks of shaggy skins, leathern armor, wolf-crowned helmets, and barbaric decorations, and the royal children shrunk from them in terror, even as they watched them with wondering curiosity. Imperial guards, gleaming in golden armor, accompanied them, while with the envoys came also as escort a small retinue of Hunnish spearmen. And in the company of these, the Princess Pulcheria noted a lad of ten or twelve years—short, swarthy, big-headed, and flat-nosed, like his brother barbarians, but with an air of open and hostile superiority that would not be moved even by all the glow and glitter of an imperial court.

Then Eslaw, the chief of the envoys of King Ruas the Hun, made known his master's demands : So much land, so much treasure, so much in the way of concession and power over the lands along the Danube, or Ruas the king would sweep down with his warriors, and lay waste the cities and lands of the empire.

"These be bold words," said Anthemius the prefect. "And what if our lord the emperor shall say thee nay ?"

But ere the chief of the envoys could reply, the lad whose presence in the escort the Princess Pulcheria had noted, sprang into the circle before the throne, brandishing his long spear in hot defiance.

" Dogs and children of dogs, ye dare not say us nay !" he cried harshly. " Except we be made the friends and allies of the emperor, and are given full store of southern gold and treasure, Ruas the king shall overturn these your palaces, and make you all captives and slaves. It shall be war between you and us forever. Thus saith my spear !"

And as he spoke he dashed his long spear upon the floor, until the mosaic pavement rang again.

Boy emperor and princesses, prefect and nobles and imperial guards, sprang to their feet as the spear clashed on the pavement, and even the barbarian envoys, while they smiled grimly at their young comrade's energy, pulled him hastily back.

But ere the prefect Anthemius could sufficiently master his astonishment to reply, the young Princess Pulcheria faced the savage envoys, and pointing to the cause of the disturbance, asked calmly :

" Who is this brawling boy, and what doth he here in the palace of the emperor ? "

And the boy made instant and defiant answer :

" I am Attila, the son of Mundzuk, kinsman to Ruas the king, and deadly foe to Rome."

"Good Anthemius," said the clear, calm voice of the unterrified girl, "were it not wise to tell this wild young prince from the northern forest that the great emperor hath gold for his friends, but only iron for his foes? 'T is ever better to be friend than foe. Bid, I pray, that the arras of the Hippodrome be parted, and let our guests see the might and power of our arms."

With a look of pleased surprise at this bold stroke of the Princess, the prefect clapped his hands in command, and the heavily brocaded curtain that screened the gilded columns parted as if by unseen hands, and the Hunnish envoys, with a gaze of stolid wonder, looked down upon the great Hippodrome of Constantinople.

It was a vast enclosure, spacious enough for the marshalling of an army. Around its sides ran tiers of marble seats, and all about it rose gleaming statues of marble, of bronze, of silver, and of gold— Augustus and the emperors, gods and goddesses of the old pagan days, heroes of the eastern and western empires. The bright oriental sun streamed down upon it, and as the trumpets sounded from beneath the imperial balcony, there filed into the arena the glittering troops of the empire, gorgeous in color and appointments, with lofty crests and gleaming armor, with shimmering spear-tips, prancing horses, towering elephants, and mighty engines

"IT SHALL BE WAR BETWEEN YOU AND US FOREVER."

of war and siege, with archers and spearmen, with
sounding trumpets and swaying standards and, high
over all, the purple *labarum*, woven in gold and
jewels,—the sacred banner of Constantine. March-
ing and counter-marching, around and around, and
in and out, until it seemed wellnigh endless, the
martial procession passed before the eyes of the
northern barbarians, watchful of every movement,
eager as children to witness this royal review.

"These are but as a handful of dust amid the
sands of the sea to the troops of the empire," said
the prefect Anthemius, when the glittering rear-
guard had passed from the Hippodrome. And the
Princess Pulcheria added, "And these, O men from
the north, are to help and succor the friends of the
great emperor, even as they are for the terror and
destruction of his foes. Bid the messengers from
Ruas the king consider, good Anthemius, whether
it were not wiser for their master to be the friend
rather than the foe of the emperor. Ask him whether
it would not be in keeping with his valor and his
might to be made one of the great captains of the
empire, with a yearly stipend of many pounds of
gold, as the recompense of the emperor for his
services and his love."

Again the prefect looked with pleasure and surprise upon this wise young girl of fifteen, who had
seen so shrewdly and so well the way to the hearts

of these northern barbarians, to whom gold and warlike display were as meat and drink.

" You hear the words of this wise young maid," he said. " Would it not please Ruas the king to be the friend of the emperor, a general of the em-pire, and the acceptor, on each recurring season of the Circensian games, of full two hundred pounds of gold as recompense for service and friendship ?"

" Say, rather, three hundred pounds," said Eslaw, the chief of the envoys, " and our master may, per-chance, esteem it wise and fair."

" Nay, it is not for the great emperor to chaffer with his friends," said Pulcheria, the princess. " Bid that the stipend be fixed at three hundred and fifty pounds of gold, good Anthemius, and let our guests bear to Ruas the king pledges and tokens of the emperor's friendship."

" And bid, too, that they do leave yon barbarian boy at our court as hostage of their faith," de-manded young Theodosius the emperor, now speaking for the first time and making a most stupid blunder at a critical moment.

For, with a sudden start of revengeful indigna-tion, young Attila the Hun turned to the boy em-peror: " I will be no man's hostage," he cried. " Freely I came, freely will I go ! Come down from thy bauble of a chair and thou and I will try, even in your circus yonder, which is the better boy, and which should rightly be hostage for faith and promise given ! "

" How now ! " exclaimed the boy emperor, altogether unused to such uncourtier-like language ; " this to me ! " And the hasty young Hun continued:

" Ay, this and more ! I tell thee, boy, that were I Ruas the king, the grass should never grow where the hoofs of my war-horse trod ; Scythia should be mine; Persia should be mine; Rome should be mine. And look you, sir emperor, the time shall surely come when the king of the Huns shall be content not with paltry tribute and needless office, but with naught but Roman treasure and Roman slaves ! "

But into this torrent of words came Pulcheria's calm voice again. " Nay, good Attila, and nay, my brother and my lord," she said. " 'T were not between friends and allies to talk of tribute, nor of slaves, nor yet of hostage. Freely did'st thou come and as freely shalt thou go ; and let this pledge tell of friendship between Theodosius the emperor and Ruas the king." And, with a step forward, she flung her own broad chain of gold around the stout and swarthy neck of the defiant young Attila.

So, through a girl's ready tact and quiet speech, was the terror of ba.barian invasion averted. Ruas the Hun rested content for years with his annual salary of three hundred and fifty pounds of gold, or over seventy thousand dollars, and his title of Gen

eral of the Empire ; while not for twenty years did
the hot-headed young Attila make good his threat
against the Roman power.

Anthemius the prefect, like the wise man he was,
recognized the worth of the young Princess Pulcheria ; he saw how great was her influence over her
brother the emperor, and noted with astonishment
and pleasure her words of wisdom and her rare
common-sense.

"Rule thou in my place, O Princess !" he said,
soon after this interview with the barbarian envoys.
"Thou alone, of all in this broad empire, art best
fitted to take lead and direction in the duties of its
governing."

Pulcheria, though a wise young girl, was prudent
and conscientious.

'Such high authority is not for a girl like me,
good Anthemius," she replied. "Rather let me
shape the ways and the growth of the emperor my
brother, and teach him how best to maintain himself in a deportment befitting his high estate, so
that he may become a wise and just ruler ; but do
thou bear sway for him until such time as he may
take the guidance on himself."

"Nay, not so, Princess," the old prefect said.
"She who can shape the ways of a boy may guide
the will of an empire. Be thou, then, Regent and
Augusta, and rule this empire as becometh the

daughter of Arcadius and the granddaughter of the great Theodosius."

And as he desired, so it was decided. The Sen-ate of the East decreed it and, in long procession, over flower-strewn pavements and through gorgeous-ly decorated streets, with the trumpets sounding their loudest, with swaying standards, and rank upon rank of imperial troops, with great officers of the government and throngs of palace attendants, this young girl of sixteen, on the fourth day of July, in the year 414, proceeded to the Church of the Holy Apostles, and was there publicly proclaimed *Pulcheria Augusta*, Regent of the East, solemnly accepting the trust as a sacred and patriotic duty.

And, not many days after, before the high altar of this same Church of the Holy Apostles, Pulche-ria the princess stood with her younger sisters, Arcadia and Marina, and with all the impressive ceremonial of the Eastern Church, made a solemn vow to devote their lives to the keeping of their father's heritage and the assistance of their only brother ; to forswear the world and all its allure-ments ; never to marry ; and to be in all things faithful and constant to each other in this their promise and their pledge.

And they were faithful and constant. The story of those three determined young maidens, yet scarcely "in their teens," reads almost like a page

PULCHERIA AUGUSTA, REGENT OF THE EAST.

from Tennyson's beautiful poem, " The Princess,"
with which many of my girl readers are doubtless
familiar.   The young regent and her sisters, with
their train of attendant maidens, renounced the
vanity of dress—wearing only plain and simple
robes ; they spent their time in making garments
for the poor, and embroidered work for church
decorations ; and with song and prayer and frugal
meals, interspersed with frequent fasts, they kept
their vow to " forswear the world and its allure-
ments," in an altogether strict and monotonous
manner.   Of course this style of living is no more
to be recommended to healthy, hearty, fun-loving
girls of fifteen than is its extreme of gayety and in-
dulgence, but it had its effect in those bad old days
of dissipation and excess, and the simplicity and
soberness of this wise young girl's life in the very
midst of so much power and luxury, made even the
worst elements in the empire respect and honor
her.

It would be interesting, did space permit, to sketch
at length some of the devisings and doings of this
girl regent of sixteen.   " She superintended with
extraordinary wisdom," says the old chronicler
Sozemon, " the transactions of the Roman government," and " afforded the spectacle," says Oz-
anam, a later historian, " of a girlish princess of
sixteen, granddaughter and sole inheritor of the

genius and courage of Theodosius the Great, governing the empires of the east and west, and being proclaimed on the death of her brother, *Augusta, Imperatrix*, and mistress of the world !"

This last event—the death of Theodosius the Younger—occurred in the year 449, and Pulcheria ascended the golden throne of Constantinople—the first woman that ever ruled as sole empress of the Roman world.

She died July 18, 453. That same year saw the death of her youthful acquaintance, Attila the Hun, that fierce barbarian whom men had called the "Scourge of God." His mighty empire stretched from the great wall of China to the Western Alps; but, though he ravaged the lands of both eastern and western Rome, he seems to have been so managed or controlled by the wise and peaceful measures of the girl regent, that his destroying hordes never troubled the splendid city by the Golden Horn which offered so rare and tempting a booty.

It is not given to the girls of to-day to have any thing like the magnificent opportunities of the young Pulcheria. But duty in many a form faces them again and again, while not unfrequently the occasion comes for sacrifice of comfort or for devotion to a trust. To all such the example of this fair young princess of old Constantinople, who, fifteen centuries ago, saw her duty plainly and undertook it simply and without hesitation, comes to strengthen and incite ; and the girl who feels herself overwhelmed by responsibility, or who is fearful of her own untried powers, may gather strength, courage, wisdom, and will from the story of this historic girl of the long ago—the wise young Regent of the East, Pulcheria of Constantinople.

Clotilda of Burgundy
The Girl of the French Vineyards

[*Afterward known as* "*St. Clotilda*," *the first Queen of France.*]
A.D. 485.

IT was little more than fourteen
hundred years ago, in the year
of our Lord 485, that a little
girl crouched trembling and
terrified, at the feet of a pity-
ing priest in the palace of the
kings of Burgundy.   There has
been many a sad little maid of ten, before and since
the days of the fair-haired Princess Clotilda, but
surely none had greater cause for terror and tears
than she.   For her cruel uncle, Gundebald, waging
war against his brother Chilperic, the rightful king of
Burgundy, had with a band of savage followers burst
into his brother's palace and, after the fierce and relentless fashion of those cruel days, had murdered

King Chilperic, the father of little Clotilda, the queen, her mother, and the young princes, her brothers; and was now searching for her and her sister Sedelenda, to kill them also.

Poor Sedelenda had hidden away in some other far-off corner; but even as Clotilda hung for protection to the robe of the good stranger-priest Ugo of Rheims (whom the king, her father, had lodged in the palace, on his homeward journey from Jerusalem), the clash of steel drew nearer and nearer. Through the corridor came the rush of feet, the arras in the doorway was rudely flung aside, and the poor child's fierce pursuers, with her cruel uncle at their head, rushed into the room.

"Hollo! Here hides the game!" he cried in savage exultation. "Thrust her away, Sir Priest, or thou diest in her stead. Not one of the tyrant's brood shall live. I say it!"

"And who art thou to judge of life or death?" demanded the priest sternly, as he still shielded the trembling child.

"I am Gundebald, King of Burgundy by the grace of mine own good sword and the right of succession," was the reply. "Trifle not with me, Sir Priest, but thrust away the child. She is my lawful prize to do with as I will. Ho, Sigebert, drag her forth!"

Quick as a flash the brave priest stepped before

the cowering child, and, with one hand still resting protectingly on the girl's fair hair, he raised the other in stern and fearless protest, and boldly faced the murderous throng.

" Back, men of blood !" he cried. " Back ! Nor dare to lay hand on this young maid who hath here sought sanctuary !" *

Fierce and savage men always respect bravery in others. There was something so courageous and heroic in the act of that single priest in thus facing a ferocious and determined band, in defence of a little girl,—for girls were but slightingly regarded in those far-off days,—that it caught the savage fancy of the cruel king. And this, joined with his respect for the Church's right of sanctuary, and with the lessening of his thirst for blood, now that he had satisfied his first desire for revenge, led him to desist.

" So be it then," he said, lowering his threatening sword. " I yield her to thee, Sir Priest. Look to her welfare and thine own. Surely a girl can do no harm."

But King Gundebald and his house lived to learn how far wrong was that unguarded statement. For the very lowering of the murderous sword that thus brought life to the little Princess Clotilda

* Under the Goths and Franks the protection of churches and priests, when extended to persons in peril, was called the " right of sanctuary," and was respected even by the fiercest of pursuers.

meant the downfall of the kingdom of Burgundy and the rise of the great and victorious nation of France. The memories of even a little maid of ten are not easily blotted out.

Her sister, Sedelenda, had found refuge and safety in the convent of Ainay, near at hand, and there, too, Clotilda would have gone, but her uncle, the new king, said: " No, the maidens must be forever separated." He expressed a willingness, however, to have the Princess Clotilda brought up in his palace, which had been her father's, and requested the priest Ugo of Rheims to remain awhile, and look after the girl's education. In those days a king's request was a command, and the good Ugo, though stern and brave in the face of real danger, was shrewd enough to know that it was best for him to yield to the king's wishes. So he continued in the palace of the king, looking after the welfare of his little charge, until suddenly the girl took matters into her own hands, and decided his future and her own.

The kingdom of Burgundy, in the days of the Princess Clotilda, was a large tract of country now embraced by Southern France and Western Switzerland. It had been given over by the Romans to the Goths, who had invaded it in the year 413. It was a land of forest and vineyards, of fair valleys and sheltered hill-sides, and of busy cities that the fostering hand of Rome had beautified; while through its broad domain the Rhone, pure and sparkling, swept with a rapid current from Swiss lake and glacier, southward to the broad and beautiful Mediterranean. Lyons was its capital, and on the hill of Fourviere, overlooking the city below it, rose the marble palace of the Burgundian kings, near to the spot where, to-day, the ruined forum of the old Roman days is still shown to tourists.

It had been a palace for centuries. Roman governors of "Imperial Gaul" had made it their head-quarters and their home; three Roman emperors had cooed and cried as babies within its walls; and it had witnessed also many a feast and foray, and the changing fortunes of Roman, Gallic, and Burgundian conquerors and over-lords. But it was no longer "home" to the little Princess Clotilda. She thought of her father and mother, and of her brothers, the little princes with whom she had played in this very palace, as it now seemed to her, so many years ago. And the more she feared her cruel uncle, the more did she desire to go far, far away from his presence. So, after thinking the whole matter over, as little girls of ten can sometimes think, she told her good friend Ugo, the priest, of her father's youngest brother Godegesil, who ruled the dependent principality of Geneva, far up the valley of the Rhone.

"Yes, child, I know the place," said Ugo. "A fair city indeed, on the blue and beautiful Lake Lemanus, walled in by mountains, and rich in corn and vineyards."

"Then let us fly thither," said the girl. "My uncle Godegesil I know will succor us, and I shall be freed from my fears of King Gundebald."

Though it seemed at first to the good priest only a child's desire, he learned to think better of it when he saw how unhappy the poor girl was in the hated palace, and how slight were her chances for improvement. And so, one fair spring morning in the year 486, the two slipped quietly out of the palace; and by slow and cautious stages, with help from friendly priests and nuns, and frequent rides in the heavy ox-wagons that were the only means of transport other than horseback, they finally reached the old city of Geneva.

And on the journey, the good Ugo had made the road seem less weary, and the lumbering ox-wagons less jolty and painful, by telling his bright young charge of all the wonders and relics he had seen in his journeyings in the East; but especially did the girl love to hear him tell of the boy king of the Franks, Hlodo-wig, or Clovis, who lived in the priest's own boyhood home of Tournay, in far-off Belgium, and who, though so brave and daring, was still a pagan, when all the world was fast becoming Christian.

And as Clotilda listened, she wished that she could turn this brave young chief away from his heathen deities, Thor and Odin, to the worship of the Christians' God ; and, revolving strange fancies in her mind, she determined what she would do when she "grew up,"—as many a girl since her day has determined. But even as they reached the fair city of Geneva—then half Roman, half Gallic, in its buildings and its life—the wonderful news met them how this boy-king Clovis, sending a challenge to combat to the prefect Syagrius, the last of the Roman governors, had defeated him in a battle at Soissons, and broken forever the power of Rome in Gaul.

War, which is never any thing but terrible, was doubly so in those savage days, and the plunder of the captured cities and homesteads was the chief return for which the barbarian soldiers followed their leaders. But when the Princess Clotilda heard how, even in the midst of his burning and plundering, the young Frankish chief spared some of the fairest Christian churches, he became still more her hero ; and again the desire to convert him from paganism and to revenge her father's murder took shape in her mind. For, devout and good though she was, this excellent little maiden of the year 485 was by no means the gentle-hearted girl of 1888, and, like most of the world about her, had but two desires : to become a good church-helper, and to be revenged on her enemies.   Certainly, fourteen centuries of progress and education have made us more loving and less vindictive.

But now that the good priest Ugo of Rheims saw that his own home land was in trouble, he felt that there lay his duty.   And Godegesil, the under-king of Geneva, feeling uneasy alike from the nearness of this boy conqueror and the possible displeasure of his brother and over-lord, King Gundebald, declined longer to shelter his niece in his palace at Geneva.

"And why may I not go with you ? " the girl asked of Ugo ; but the old priest knew that a conquered and plundered land was no place to which to convey a young maid for safety, and the princess, therefore, found refuge among the sisters of the church of St. Peter in Geneva.   And here she passed her girlhood, as the record says, "in works of piety and charity."

So four more years went by.   In the north, the boy chieftain, reaching manhood, had been raised aloft on the shields of his fair-haired and long-limbed followers, and with many a "haël!" and shout had been proclaimed "King of the Franks." In the south, the young Princess Clotilda, now nearly sixteen, had washed the feet of pilgrims, ministered to the poor, and, after the manner of her day, had proved herself a zealous church-worker in that low-roofed convent near the old church of St. Peter, high on that same hill in Geneva where to-day, hemmed in by narrow streets and tall houses, the cathedral of St. Peter, twice re-builded since Clotilda's time, overlooks the quaint city, the beautiful lake of Geneva, and the rushing Rhone, and sees across the valley of the Arve the gray and barren rocks of the Petit Séléve and the distant snows of Mont Blanc.

One bright summer day, as the young princess passed into the *hospitium*, or guest-room for poor pilgrims, attached to the convent, she saw there a stranger, dressed in rags. He had the wallet and staff of a mendicant, or begging pilgrim, and, coming toward her, he asked for " charity in the name of the blessed St. Peter, whose church thou servest."

The young girl brought the pilgrim food, and then, according to the custom of the day, kneeling on the earthen floor, she began to bathe his feet. But as she did so, the pilgrim, bending forward, said in a low voice :

" Lady, I have·great matters to announce to thee, if thou deign to permit me to reveal them."

Pilgrims in those days were frequently made the bearers of special messages between distant friends ; but this poor young orphan princess could think of

no one from whom a message to her might come.
Nevertheless, she simply said : " Say on."

In the same low tone the beggar continued :
" Clovis, King of the Franks, sends thee greeting."

The girl looked up now, thoroughly surprised.
This beggar must be a madman, she thought.
But the eyes of the pilgrim looked at her reassur-
ingly, and he said : " In token whereof, he sendeth
thee this ring by me, his confidant and *comitatus*,*
Aurelian of Soissons."

The Princess Clotilda took, as if in a dream, the
ring of transparent jacinth set in solid gold, and
asked quietly :

" What would the king of the Franks with
me ? "

" The king, my master, hath heard from the holy
Bishop Remi and the good priest Ugo of thy
beauty and discreetness," replied Aurelian ; " and
likewise of the sad condition of one who is the
daughter of a royal line. He bade me use all my
wit to come nigh to thee, and to say that, if it be
the will of the gods, he would fain raise thee to his
rank by marriage."

Those were days of swift and sudden surprises,
when kings made up their minds in royal haste,
and princesses were not expected to be surprised at

---

* One of the king's special body-guard, from which comes the title *comp*,
or count.

CLOTILDA AND THE PILGRIM.

whatever they might hear. And so we must not
feel surprised to learn that all the dreams of her
younger days came into the girl's mind, and that,
as the record states, "she accepted the ring with
great joy."

"Return promptly to thy lord," she said to the
messenger, "and bid him, if he would fain unite
me to him in marriage, to send messengers without
delay to demand me of my uncle, King Gundebald, and let those same messengers take me away
in haste, so soon as they shall have obtained permission."

For this wise young princess knew that her uncle's
word was not to be long depended upon, and she
feared, too, that certain advisers at her uncle's court
might counsel him to do her harm before the messengers of King Clovis could have conducted her
beyond the borders of Burgundy.

Aurelian, still in his pilgrim's disguise, for he
feared discovery in a hostile country, hastened
back to King Clovis, who, the record says, was
"pleased with his success and with Clotilda's no-
tion, and at once sent a deputation to Gundebald
to demand his niece in marriage."

As Clotilda foresaw, her uncle stood in too much
dread of this fierce young conqueror of the north
to say him nay. And soon in the palace at Lyons,
so full of terrible memories to this orphan girl, the

courteous Aurelian, now no longer in beggar's rags,
but gorgeous in white silk and a flowing *sagum,* or
mantle of vermilion, publicly engaged himself, as
the representative of King Clovis, to the Princess
Clotilda ; and, according to the curious custom of
the time, cemented the engagement by giving to
the young girl a *sou* and a *denier.**

" Now deliver the princess into our hand, O
king," said the messenger, " that we may take
her to King Clovis, who waiteth for us even now
at Chalons to conclude these nuptials."

So, almost before he knew what he was doing,
King Gundebald had bidden his niece farewell ;
and the princess, with her escort of Frankish
spears, was rumbling away in a clumsy *basterne,*
or covered ox-wagon, toward the frontier of Burgundy.

But the slow-moving ox-wagon by no means
suited the impatience of this shrewd young princess. She knew her uncle, the king of Burgundy,
too well. When once he was roused to action, he
was fierce and furious.

" Good Aurelian," she said at length to the
king's ambassador, who rode by her side : " if
that thou wouldst take me into the presence of
thy lord, the king of the Franks, let me descend

---

* Two pieces of old French coin, equalling about a cent and a mill in
American money.

from this carriage, mount me on horseback, and let
us speed hence as fast as we may, for never in this
carriage shall I reach the presence of my lord, the
king."

And none too soon was her advice acted upon ;
for the counsellors of King Gundebald, noticing
Clotilda's anxiety to be gone, concluded that, after
all, they had made a mistake in betrothing her to
King Clovis.

" Thou shouldst have remembered, my lord,"
they said, " that thou didst slay Clotilda's father,
her mother, and the young princes, her brothers.
If Clotilda become powerful, be sure she will
avenge the wrong thou hast wrought her."

And forthwith the king sent off an armed band,
with orders to bring back both the princess and
the treasure he had sent with her as her marriage
portion. But already the princess and her escort
were safely across the Seine, where, in the Cam-
pania, or plain - country, — later known as the
province of Champagne — she met the king of
the Franks.

I am sorry to be obliged to confess that the first
recorded desire of this beautiful, brave, and devout young maiden, when she found herself safely
among the fierce followers of King Clovis, was a
request for vengeance. But we must remember,
girls and boys, that this is a story of half-savage

days when, as I have already said, the desire for
revenge on one's enemies was common to all.

From the midst of his skin-clad and green-robed
guards and nobles, young Clovis—in a dress of
" crimson and gold, and milk-white silk," and with
his yellow hair coiled in a great top-knot on his
uncovered head—advanced to meet his bride.

" My lord king," said Clotilda, " the bands of
the king of Burgundy follow hard upon us to bear
me off. Command, I pray thee, that these, my escort, scatter themselves right and left for twoscore
miles, and plunder and burn the lands of the king
of Burgundy."

Probably in no other way could this wise young
girl of seventeen have so thoroughly pleased the
fierce and warlike young king. He gladly ordered
her wishes to be carried out, and the plunderers
forthwith departed to carry out the royal command.

So her troubles were ended, and this prince
and princess,—Hlodo-wig, or Clovis (meaning the
" warrior youth "), and Hlodo-hilde, or Clotilda
(meaning the " brilliant and noble maid "),—in
spite of the wicked uncle Gundebald, were married
at Soissons, in the year 493, and, as the fairy stories
say, " lived happily together ever after."

The record of their later years has no place in
this sketch of the girlhood of Clotilda ; but it is one
of the most interesting and dramatic of the old-

time historic stories. The dream of that sad little princess in the old convent at Geneva, "to make her boy-hero a Christian, and to be revenged on the murderer of her parents," was in time fulfilled. For on Christmas-day, in the year 493, the young king and three thousand of his followers were baptized amid gorgeous ceremonial in the great church of St. Martin at Rheims.

The story of the young queen's revenge is not to be told in these pages. But, though terrible, it is only one among the many tales of vengeance that show us what fierce and cruel folk our ancestors were, in the days when passion instead of love ruled the hearts of men and women, and of boys and girls as well; and how favored are we of this nineteenth century, in all the peace and prosperity and home happiness that surround us.

But from this conversion, as also from this revenge, came the great power of Clovis and Clotilda; for, ere his death, in the year 511, he brought all the land under his sway from the Rhine to the Rhone, the ocean and the Pyrenees; he was hailed by his people with the old Roman titles of Consul and Augustus, and reigned victorious as the first king of France. Clotilda, after years of wise counsel and charitable works, upon which her determination for revenge seems to be the only stain, died long after her husband, in the year

PRINCESS CLOTILDA'S JOURNEY.

545, and to-day, in the city of Paris, which was even then the capital of new France, the church of St. Clotilda stands as her memorial, while her marble statue may be seen by the traveller in the great palace of the Luxembourg.

A typical girl of those harsh old days of the long ago,—loving and generous toward her friends, unforgiving and revengeful to her enemies,—reared in the midst of cruelty and of charity, she did her duty according to the light given her, made France a Christian nation, and so helped on the progress of civilization. Certainly a place among the world's historic girls may rightly be accorded to this fair-haired young princess of the summer-land of France, the beautiful Clotilda of Burgundy.

WOO OF HWANG-HO.

THE GIRL OF THE YELLOW RIVER.

[Afterwards the Great Empress Woo of China.]
A.D. 635.

THOMAS the Nestorian had been in many lands and in the midst of many dangers, but he had never before found himself in quite so unpleasant a position as now. Six ugly Tartar horsemen with very uncomfortable-looking spears and appalling shouts, and mounted on their swift Kirghiz ponies, were charging down upon him, while neither the rushing Yellow River on the right hand, nor the steep dirt-cliffs on the left, could offer him shelter or means of escape. These dirt-cliffs, or "loess," to give them their scientific name, are remarkable banks of brownish-yellow loam,

79

found largely in Northern and Western China, and rising sometimes to a height of a thousand feet. Their peculiar yellow tinge makes every thing look "hwang" or yellow,—and hence yellow is a favorite color among the Chinese. So, for instance, the emperor is "Hwang-ti"— the "Lord of the Yellow Land"; the imperial throne is the "Hwang-wei" or "yellow throne" of China; the great river, formerly spelled in your school geographies Hoang-ho, is "Hwang-ho," the "yellow river," etc.

These "hwang" cliffs, or dirt-cliffs, are full of caves and crevices, but the good priest could see no convenient cave, and he had therefore no alternative but to boldly face his fate, and like a brave man calmly meet what he could not avoid.

But, just as he had singled out, as his probable captor, one peculiarly unattractive-looking horseman, whose crimson sheepskin coat and long horse-tail plume were streaming in the wind, and just as he had braced himself to meet the onset against the great "loess," or dirt-cliff, he felt a twitch at his black upper robe, and a low voice—a girl's, he was confident—said quickly:

"Look not before nor behind thee, good O-lo-pun, but trust to my word and give a backward leap."

Thomas the Nestorian had learned two valuable

lessons in his much wandering about the earth,—
never to appear surprised, and always to be ready
to act quickly. So, knowing nothing of the possible results of his action, but feeling that it could
scarcely be worse than death from Tartar spears,
he leaped back, as bidden.

The next instant, he found himself flat upon his
back in one of the low-ceiled cliff caves that abound
in Western China, while the screen of vines that had
concealed its entrance still quivered from his fall.
Picking himself up and breathing a prayer of
thanks for his deliverance, he peered through the
leafy doorway and beheld in surprise six much astonished Tartar robbers regarding with looks of
puzzled wonder a defiant little Chinese girl, who
had evidently darted out of the cave as he had
tumbled in. She was facing the enemy as boldly
as had he, and her little almond eyes fairly danced
with mischievous delight at their perplexity.

At once he recognized the child. She was Woo
(the "high-spirited" or "dauntless one"), the
bright young girl whom he had often noticed in
the throng at his mission-house in Tûng-Chow,—
the little city by the Yellow River, where her father,
the bannerman, held guard at the Dragon Gate.

He was about to call out to the girl to save herself, when, with a sudden swoop, the Tartar whom
he had braced himself to resist, bent in his saddle

and made a dash for the child. But agile little
Woo was quicker than the Tartar horseman.
With a nimble turn and a sudden spring, she
dodged the Tartar's hand, darted under his pony's
legs, and with a shrill laugh of derision, sprang
up the sharp incline, and disappeared in one of the
many cliff caves before the now doubly baffled
horsemen could see what had become of her.

With a grunt of discomfiture and disgust, the
Tartar riders turned their ponies' heads and galloped off along the road that skirted the yellow
waters of the swift-flowing Hwang-ho. Then a little yellow face peeped out of a cave farther up the
cliff, a black-haired, tightly braided head bobbed
and twitched with delight, and the next moment
the good priest was heartily thanking his small
ally for so skilfully saving him from threatened
capture.

It was a cool September morning in the days of
the great Emperor Tai, twelve hundred and fifty
years ago. And a great emperor was Tai-tsûng,
though few, if any, of my young readers ever heard
his name. His splendid palace stood in the midst
of lovely gardens in the great city of Chang-an,—
that old, old city that for over two thousand years
was the capital of China, and which you can now
find in your geographies under its modern name of
Singan-foo. And in the year 635, when our story

AGILE LITTLE WOO WAS QUICKER THAN THE TARTAR HORSEMAN.

opens, the name of Tai-tsûng was great and powerful throughout the length and breadth of Chûng
Kwoh—the "Middle Kingdom," as the Chinese for
nearly thirty centuries have called their vast
country—while the stories of his fame and power
had reached to the western courts of India and of
Persia, of Constantinople, and even of distant Rome.

It was a time of darkness and strife in Europe.
Already what historians have called the Dark
Ages had settled upon the Christian world. And
among all the races of men the only nation that
was civilized, and learned, and cultivated, and refined in this seventh century of the Christian era,
was this far eastern Empire of China, where
schools and learning flourished, and arts and man-
ufactures abounded, when America was as yet un-
discovered and Europe was sunk in degradation.

And here, since the year 505, the Nestorians, a
branch of the Christian Church, originating in
Asia Minor in the fifth century, and often called
"the Protestants of the East," had been spreading the story of the life and love of Christ. And
here, in this year of grace 635, in the city of
Chang-an, and in all the region about the Yellow
River, the good priest Thomas the Nestorian,
whom the Chinese called O-lo-pun—the nearest
approach they could give to his strange Syriac
name- -had his Christian mission-house, and was

zealously bringing to the knowledge of a great
and enlightened people the still greater and more
helpful light of Christianity.

"My daughter," said the Nestorian after his
words of thanks were uttered ; "this is a gracious
deed done to me, and one that I may not easily
repay. Yet would I gladly do so, if I might. Tell
me what wouldst thou like above all other things?"

The answer of the girl was as ready as it was un-
pected.

"To be a boy, O master!" she replied. "Let
the great Shang-ti,* whose might thou teachest,
make me a man that I may have revenge."

The good priest had found strange things in his
mission work in this far Eastern land, but this
wrathful demand of an excited little maid was full
as strange as any. For China is and ever has been
a land in which the chief things taught the children
are, " subordination, passive submission to the law,
to parents, and to all superiors, and a peaceful de-
meanor."

" Revenge is not for men to trifle with, nor maids
to talk of," he said. " Harbor no such desires, but
rather come with me and I will show thee more
attractive things. This very day doth the great
emperor go forth from the City of Peace, † to the

* Almighty Being.

† The meaning of Chang-an, the ancient capital of China, is " the City of
Continuous Peace."

banks of the Yellow River. Come thou with me to witness the splendor of his train, and perchance even to see the great emperor himself and the young Prince Kaou, his son."

"That I will not then," cried the girl, more hotly than before. " I hate this great emperor, as men do wrongfully call him, and I hate the young Prince Kaou. May Lûng Wang, the god of the dragons, dash them both beneath the Yellow River ere yet they leave its banks this day."

At this terrible wish on the lips of a girl, the good master very nearly forgot even his most valuable precept—never to be surprised. He regarded his defiant young companion in sheer amazement.

" Have a care, have a care, my daughter ! " he said at length. " The blessed Saint James telleth us that the tongue is a little member, but it can kindle a great fire. How mayst thou hope to say such direful words against the Son of Heaven * and live ? "

The Son of Heaven killed the emperor, my father," said the child.

"The emperor thy father ! " Thomas the Nestorian almost gasped in this latest surprise. " Is the girl crazed or doth she sport with one who seeketh her good?" And amazement and perplexity settled upon his face.

* " The Son of Heaven " is one of the chief titles of the Chinese emperor.

" The Princess Woo is neither crazed nor doth she sport with the master," said the girl. " I do but speak the truth. Great is Tai-tsûng. Whom he will he slayeth, and whom he will he keepeth alive." And then she told the astonished priest that the bannerman of the Dragon Gate was not her father at all. For, she said, as she had lain awake only the night before, she had heard enough in talk between the bannerman and his wife to learn her secret—how that she was the only daughter of the rightful emperor, the Prince Kûng-ti, whose guardian and chief adviser the present emperor had been ; how this trusted protector had made away with poor Kûng-ti in order that he might usurp the throne ; and how she, the Princess Woo, had been flung into the swift Hwang-ho, from the turbid waters of which she had been rescued by the bannerman of the Dragon Gate.

" This may or may not be so," Thomas the Nestorian said, uncertain whether or not to credit the girl's surprising story ; " but even were it true, my daughter, how couldst thou right thyself ? What can a girl hope to do ? "

The young princess drew up her small form proudly. " Do ? " she cried in brave tones ; " I can do much, wise O-lo-pun, girl though I am ! Did not a girl save the divine books of Confucius, when the great Emperor Chi-Hwang-ti did command the

burning of all the books in the empire ? Did not a
girl — though but a soothsayer's daughter — raise
the outlaw Liû Pang straight to the Yellow
Throne? And shall I, who am the daughter of
emperors, fail to be as able or as brave as they?"

The wise Nestorian was shrewd enough to see
that here was a prize that might be worth the fostering. By the assumption of mystic knowledge,
he learned from the bannerman of the Dragon
Gate, the truth of the girl's story, and so worked
upon the good bannerman's native superstition and
awe of superior power as to secure the custody of
the young princess, and to place her in his mission-
house at Tûng-Chow for teaching and guidance.
Among the early Christians, the Nestorians held
peculiarly helpful and elevating ideas of the worth
and proper condition of woman. Their precepts
were full of mutual help, courtesy, and fraternal
love. All these the Princess Woo learned under
her preceptor's guidance. She grew to be even
more assertive and self-reliant, and became, also,
expert in many sports in which, in that woman-
despising country, only boys could hope to excel.

One day, when she was about fourteen years old,
the Princess Woo was missing from the Nestorian
mission-house, by the Yellow River. Her troubled
guardian, in much anxiety, set out to find the
truant ; and, finally, in the course of his search,

climbed the high bluff from which he saw the massive walls, the many gateways, the gleaming roofs, and porcelain towers of the Imperial city of Chang-an—the City of Continuous Peace.

But even before he had entered its northern gate, a little maid in loose silken robe, peaked cap, and embroidered shoes had passed through that very gateway, and slipping through the thronging streets of the great city, approached at last the group of picturesque and glittering buildings that composed the palace of the great Emperor Tai.

Just within the main gateway of the palace rose the walls of the Imperial Academy, where eight thousand Chinese boys received instruction under the patronage of the emperor, while, just beyond extended the long, low range of the archery school, in which even the emperor himself sometimes came to witness, or take part in, the exciting contests.

Drawing about her shoulders the yellow sash that denoted alliance with royalty, the Princess Woo, without a moment's hesitation, walked straight through the palace gateway, past the wondering guards, and into the boundaries of the archery court.

Here the young Prince Kaou, an indolent and lazy lad of about her own age, was cruelly goading on his trained crickets to a ferocious fight within their gilded bamboo cage, while, just at hand, the slaves were preparing his bow and arrows for his daily archery practice.

Now, among the rulers of China there are three classes of privileged targets—the skin of the bear for the emperor himself, the skin of the deer for the princes of the blood, and the skin of the tiger for the nobles of the court ; and thus, side by side, in the Imperial Archery School at Chang-an, hung the three targets.

The girl with the royal sash and the determined face walked straight up to the Prince Kaou. The boy left off goading his fighting crickets, and looked in astonishment at this strange and highly audacious girl, who dared to enter a place from which all women were excluded. Before the guards could interfere, she spoke.

"Are the arrows of the great Prince Kaou so well fitted to the cord," she said, "that he dares to try his skill with one who, although a girl, hath yet the wit and right to test his skill ?"

The guards laid hands upon the intruder to drag her away, but the prince, nettled at her tone, yet glad to welcome any thing that promised novelty or amusement, bade them hold off their hands.

"No girl speaketh thus to the Prince Kaou and liveth," he said insolently. "Give me instant test of thy boast, or the wooden collar * in the palace torture-house, shall be thy fate."

* The " wooden collar " was the " kia " or " cangue,"—a terrible instrument of torture used in China for the punishment of criminals.

"Give me the arrows, Prince," the girl said, bravely, "and I will make good my words."

At a sign, the slaves handed her a bow and arrows. But, as she tried the cord and glanced along the polished shaft, the prince said :

"Yet, stay, girl ; here is no target set for thee. Let the slaves set up the people's target. These are not for such as thou."

"Nay, Prince, fret not thyself," the girl coolly replied. " My target is here ! " and while all looked on in wonder, the undaunted girl deliberately toed the practice line, twanged her bow, and with a sudden whiz, sent her well-aimed shaft quivering straight into the small white centre of the great bearskin—the imperial target itself !

With a cry of horror and of rage at such sacrilege, the guards pounced upon the girl archer, and would have dragged her away. But with the same quick motion that had saved her from the Tartar robbers, she sprang from their grasp and, standing full before the royal target, she said commandingly :

"Hands off, slaves ; nor dare to question my right to the bearskin target. I am the Empress !"

It needed but this to cap the climax. Prince, guards, and slaves looked at this extraordinary girl in open-mouthed wonder. But ere their speechless amazement could change to instant seizure, a loud laugh rang from the imperial doorway and a hearty voice exclaimed : " Braved, and by a girl ! Who is thy Empress, Prince ? Let me, too, salute the Tsih-tien !" * Then a portly figure, clad in yellow robes, strode down to the targets, while all within the archery lists prostrated themselves in homage before one of China's greatest monarchs—the Emperor Tai-tsung, Wun-woo-ti.†

But before even the emperor could reach the girl, the bamboo screen was swept hurriedly aside, and into the archery lists came the anxious priest, Thomas the Nestorian. He had traced his missing charge even to the imperial palace, and now found her in the very presence of those he deemed her mortal enemies. Prostrate at the emperor's feet, he told the young girl's story, and then pleaded for her life, promising to keep her safe and secluded in his mission-home at Tûng-Chow.

The Emperor Tai laughed a mighty laugh, for the bold front of this only daughter of his former master and rival, suited his warlike humor. But he was a wise and clement monarch withal.

" Nay, wise O-lo-pun," he said. " Such rivals to our throne may not be at large, even though sheltered in the temples of the *hûng-mao*.‡ The royal blood of the house of Sui § flows safely only within

---

* " The Sovereign Divine "—an imperial title.

† " Our Exalted Ancestor—the Literary-Martial Emperor."

‡ The "light-haired ones "—an old Chinese term for the western Christians.　　　　§ The name of the former dynasty.

"I AM THE EMPRESS!"

palace walls. Let the proper decree be registered, and let the gifts be exchanged; for to-morrow thy ward, the Princess Woo, becometh one of our most noble queens."

And so at fourteen, even as the records show. this strong-willed young girl of the Yellow River became one of the wives of the great Emperor Tai. She proved a very gracious and acceptable step-mother to young Prince Kaou, who, as the records also tell us, grew so fond of the girl queen that, within a year from the death of his great father, and when he himself had succeeded to the Yellow Throne, as Emperor Supreme, he recalled the Queen Woo from her retirement in the mission-house at Tûng-Chow and made her one of his royal wives. Five years after, in the year 655, she was declared Empress, and during the reign of her lazy and indolent husband she was "the power behind the throne." And when, in the year 683, Kaou-tsûng died, she boldly assumed the direction of the government, and, ascending the throne, de-clared herself Woo How Tsih-tien—Woo the Em-press Supreme and Sovereign Divine.

History records that this Zenobia of China proved equal to the great task. She "governed the empire with discretion," extended its borders, and was acknowledged as empress from the shores of the Pacific to the borders of Persia, of India, and of the Caspian Sea.

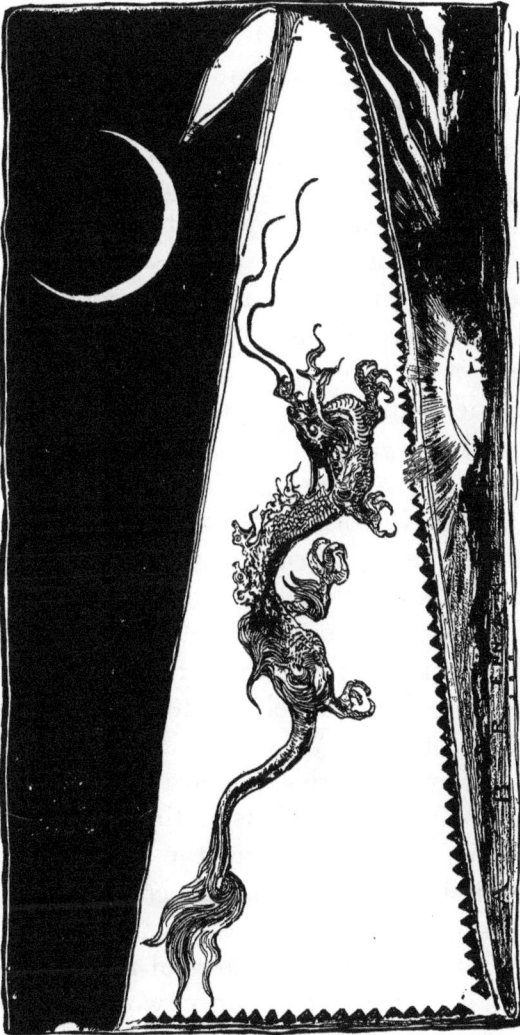

THE GOLDEN HORN.

Her reign was one of the longest and most suc
cessful in that period known in history as the
Golden Age of China. Because of the relentless
native prejudice against a successful woman, in a
country where girl babies are ruthlessly drowned,
as the quickest way of ridding the world of useless
incumbrances, Chinese historians have endeavored
to blacken her character and undervalue her services. But later scholars now see that she was a
powerful and successful queen, who did great
good to her native land, and strove to maintain its
power and glory.

She never forgot her good friend and protector,
Thomas the Nestorian. During her long reign of
almost fifty years, Christianity strengthened in the
kingdom, and obtained a footing that only the
great Mahometan conquests of five centuries later
entirely destroyed ; and the Empress Woo, so the
chronicles declare, herself " offered sacrifices to the
great God of all." When, hundreds of years after,
the Jesuit missionaries penetrated into this most
exclusive of all the nations of the earth, they found
near the palace at Chang-an the ruins of the Nestorian mission church, with the cross still standing,
and, preserved through all the changes of dynasties,
an abstract in Syriac characters of the Christian law,
and with it the names of seventy-two attendant priests
who had served the church established by O-lo-pun.

Thus, in a land in which, from the earliest ages, women have been regarded as little else but slaves, did a self-possessed and wise young girl triumph over all difficulties, and rule over her many millions of subjects "in a manner becoming a great prince." This, even her enemies admit. "Lessening the miseries of her subjects," so the historians declare, she governed the wide Empire of China wisely, discreetly, and peacefully; and she displayed upon the throne all the daring, wit, and wisdom that had marked her actions when, years before, she was nothing but a sprightly and determined little Chinese maiden, on the banks of the turbid Yellow River.

EDITH OF SCOTLAND.

THE GIRL OF THE NORMAN ABBEY.

*[Afterward known as the " Good Queen Maud"
of England.]* A.D. 1093.

O
N a broad and deep window-seat in the old
Abbey guest-house at Gloucester, sat two
young girls of thirteen and ten ; before them,
brave-looking enough in his old-time costume, stood
a manly young fellow of sixteen.   The three were
in earnest conversation, all unmindful of the noise
about them—the romp and riot of a throng of young
folk, attendants, or followers of the knights and
barons of King William's court.

For William Rufus, son of the Conqueror and
second Norman king of England, held his Whit-
suntide *gemôt*, or summer council of his lords

and lieges, in the curious old Roman-Saxon-Norman town of Gloucester, in the fair vale through which flows the noble Severn. The city is known to the young folk of to-day as the one in which good Robert Raikes started the first Sunday-school more than a hundred years ago. But the *gemôt* of King William the Red, which was a far different gathering from good Mr. Raikes' Sunday-school, was held in the great chapter-house of the old Benedictine Abbey, while the court was lodged in the Abbey guest-houses, in the grim and fortress-like Gloucester Castle, and in the houses of the quaint old town itself.

The boy was shaking his head rather doubtfully as he stood, looking down upon the two girls on the broad window-seat.

"Nay, nay, beausire *; shake not your head like that," exclaimed the younger of the girls. "We did escape that way, trust me we did; Edith here can tell you I do speak the truth—for sure, 't was her device."

Thirteen-year-old Edith laughed merrily enough at her sister's perplexity, and said gayly as the lad turned questioningly to her:

Sure, then, beausire, 't is plain to see that you are Southron-born and know not the complexion of

---

* "Fair sir": an ancient style of address, used especially toward those high in rank in Norman times.

a Scottish mist. Yet 't is even as Mary said. For, as we have told you, the Maiden's Castle standeth high-placed on the crag in Edwin's Burgh, and hath many and devious pathways to the lower gate. So when the Red Donald's men were swarming up the steep, my uncle, the Atheling, did guide us, by ways we knew well, and by twists and turnings that none knew better, straight through Red Donald's array, and all unseen and unnoted of them, because of the blessed thickness of the gathering mist."

"And this was *your* device?" asked the boy, admiringly.

"Ay, but any one might have devised it too," replied young Edith, modestly. "Sure, 't was no great device to use a Scotch mist for our safety, and 't were wiser to chance it than stay and be stupidly murdered by Red Donald's men. And so it was, good Robert, even as Mary did say, that we came forth unharmed, from amidst them and fled here to King William's court, where we at last are safe."

"Safe, say you; safe?" exclaimed the lad, impulsively. "Ay, as safe as is a mouse's nest in a cat's ear—as safe as is a rabbit in a ferret's hutch. But that I know you to be a brave and dauntless maid, I should say to you——"

But, ere Edith could know what he would say, their conference was rudely broken in upon. For a royal page, dashing up to the three, with scant courtesy seized the arm of the elder girl, and said hurriedly :

"Haste ye, haste ye, my lady! Our lord king is even now calling for you to come before him in the banquet-hall."

Edith knew too well the rough manners of those dangerous days. She freed herself from the grasp of the page, and said :

"Nay, that may I not, master page. 'T is neither safe nor seemly for a maid to show herself in baron's hall or in king's banquet-room."

"Safe and seemly it may not be, but come you must," said the page, rudely. "The king demands it, and your nay is naught."

And so, hurried along whether she would or no, while her friend, Robert Fitz Godwine, accompanied her as far as he dared, the young Princess Edith was speedily brought into the presence of the king of England, William II., called, from the color of his hair and from his fiery temper, Rufus, or "the Red."

For Edith and Mary were both princesses of Scotland, with a history, even before they had reached their teens, as romantic as it was exciting. Their mother, an exiled Saxon princess, had, after the conquest of Saxon England by the stern Duke William the Norman, found refuge in Scotland, and

had there married King Malcolm Canmore, the son
of that King Duncan whom Macbeth had slain.
But when King Malcolm had fallen beneath the
walls of Alnwick Castle, a victim to English treachery, and when his fierce brother Donald Bane, or
Donald the Red, had usurped the throne of Scotland, then the good Queen Margaret died in the
gray castle on the rock of Edinburgh, and the five
orphaned children were only saved from the vengeance of their bad uncle Donald by the shrewd
and daring device of the young Princess Edith, who
bade their good uncle Edgar, the Atheling, guide
them, under cover of the mist, straight through the
Red Donald's knights and spearmen to England
and safety.

You would naturally suppose that the worst possible place for the fugitives to seek safety was in
Norman England ; for Edgar the Atheling, a Saxon
prince, had twice been declared king of England
by the Saxon enemies of the Norman conquerors,
and the children of King Malcolm and Queen Margaret—half Scotch, half Saxon—were, by blood and
birth, of the two races most hateful to the conquerors. But the Red King in his rough sort of
way—hot to-day and cold to-morrow—had shown
something almost like friendship for this Saxon
Atheling, or royal prince, who might have been
king of England had he not wisely submitted to

the greater power of Duke William the Conqueror
and to the Red William, his son. More than this,
it had been rumored that some two years before,
when there was truce between the kings of England and of Scotland, this harsh and headstrong
English king, who was as rough and repelling as a
chestnut burr, had seen, noticed, and expressed a
particular interest in the eleven-year-old Scottish
girl—this very Princess Edith who now sought his
protection.

So, when this wandering uncle boldly threw
himself upon Norman courtesy, and came with his
homeless nephews and nieces straight to the Norman court for safety, King William Rufus not only
received these children of his hereditary foeman
with favor and royal welcome, but gave them
comfortable lodgment in quaint old Gloucester
town, where he held his court.

But even when the royal fugitives deemed themselves safest were they in the greatest danger.

Among the attendant knights and nobles of
King William's court was a Saxon knight known
as Sir Ordgar, a " thegn," * or baronet, of Oxford-
shire ; and because those who change their opin-
ions—political or otherwise—often prove the most
unrelenting enemies of their former associates, it
came to pass that Sir Ordgar, the Saxon, conceived

* Pronounced thane.

a strong dislike for these orphaned descendants of
the Saxon kings, and convinced himself that the
best way to secure himself in the good graces of
the Norman King William was to slander and
accuse the children of the Saxon Queen Margaret.

And so that very day, in the great hall, when
wine was flowing and passions were strong, this
false knight, raising his glass, bade them all drink :
" Confusion to the enemies of our liege the king,
from the base Philip of France to the baser Edgar
the Atheling and his Scottish brats ! "

This was an insult that even the heavy and
peace-loving nature of Edgar the Atheling could
not brook.   He sprang to his feet and denounced
the charge :

" None here is truer or more leal to you, lord
king," he said, " than am I, Edgar the Atheling,
and my charges, your guests."

But King William Rufus was of that changing
temper that goes with jealousy and suspicion.   His
flushed face grew still more red, and, turning away
from the Saxon prince, he demanded :

" Why make you this charge, Sir Ordgar ? "

" Because of of its truth, beausire," said the faith-
less knight.   " For what other cause hath this false
Atheling sought sanctuary here, save to use his
own descent from the ancient kings of this realm
to make head and force among your lieges ?   And

his eldest kinsgirl here, the Princess Edith, hath she not been spreading a trumpery story among the younger folk, of how some old *wyrd-wif* * hath said that she who is the daughter of kings shall be the wife and mother of kings? And is it not further true that when her aunt, the Abbess of Romsey, bade her wear the holy veil, she hath again and yet again torn it off, and affirmed that she, who was to be a queen, could never be made a nun? Children and fools, 't is said, do speak the truth, beausire; and in all this do I see the malice and device of this false Atheling, the friend of your rebellious brother, Duke Robert, as you do know him to be; and I do brand him here, in this presence, as traitor and recreant to you, his lord."

The anger of the jealous king grew more unreasoning as Sir Ordgar went on.

"Enough!" he cried. "Seize the traitor, —— or, stay; children and fools, as you have said, Sir Ordgar, do indeed speak the truth. Have in the girl and let us hear the truth. 'Not seemly'? Sir Atheling," he broke out in reply to some protest of Edith's uncle. "Aught is seemly that the king doth wish. Holo! Raoul! Damian! sirrah pages! Run, one of you, and seek the Princess Edith, and bring her here forthwith!"

* Witch-wife or seeress,

And while Edgar the Atheling, realizing that this was the gravest of all his dangers, strove, though without effect, to reason with the angry king, Damian, the page, as we have seen, hurried after the Princess Edith.

"How now, mistress!" broke out the Red King, as the young girl was ushered into the banquet-hall, where the disordered tables, strewn with fragments of the feast, showed the ungentle manners of those brutal days. "How now, mistress! do you prate of kings and queens and of your own designs—you, who are but a beggar guest? Is it seemly or wise to talk,—nay, keep you quiet, Sir Atheling; we will have naught from you,—to talk of thrones and crowns as if you did even now hope to win the realm from me—from me, your only protector?"

The Princess Edith was a very high-spirited maiden, as all the stories of her girlhood show. And this unexpected accusation, instead of frightening her, only served to embolden her. She looked the angry monarch full in the face.

"'T is a false and lying charge, lord king," she said, "from whomsoever it may come. Naught have I said but praise of you and your courtesy to us motherless folk. 'T is a false and lying charge; and I am ready to stand test of its proving, come what may."

"'T IS A FALSE AND LYING CHARGE."

"Even to the judgment of God, girl?" demanded the king.

And the brave girl made instant reply : "Even
to the judgment of God, lord king." Then, skilled
in all the curious customs of those warlike times,
she drew off her glove. "Whosoever my accuser be,
lord king," she said, "I do denounce him as fore-
sworn and false, and thus do I throw myself upon
God's good mercy, if it shall please him to raise me
up a champion." And she flung her glove upon the
floor of the hall, in face of the king and all his barons.

It was a bold thing for a girl to do, and a mur-
mur of applause ran through even that unfriendly
throng. For, to stand the test of a "wager of
battle," or the "judgment of God," as the savage
contest was called, was the last resort of any one
accused of treason or of crime. It meant no less
than a "duel to the death" between the accuser
and the accused or their accepted champions, and,
upon the result of the duel hung the lives of those
in dispute. And the Princess Edith's glove lying
on the floor of the Abbey hall was her assertion
that she had spoken the truth and was willing to
risk her life in proof of her innocence.

Edgar the Atheling, peace-lover, though he was,
would gladly have accepted the post of champion
for his niece, but, as one also involved in the charge
of treason, such action was denied him.

For the moment, the Red King's former admiration for this brave young princess caused him to waver; but those were days when suspicion and jealousy rose above all nobler traits. His face grew stern again.

"Ordgar of Oxford," he said, "take up the glove!" and Edith knew who was her accuser. Then the King asked: "Who standeth as champion for Edgar the Atheling and this maid, his niece?"

Almost before the words were spoken young Robert Fitz Godwine had sprung to Edith's side.

"That would I, lord king, if a young squire might appear against a belted knight!"

"Ordgar of Oxford fights not with boys!" said the accuser contemptuously.

The king's savage humor broke out again.

"Face him with your own page, Sir Ordgar," he said, with a grim laugh. "Boy against boy would be a fitting wager for a young maid's life."

But the Saxon knight was in no mood for sport.

"Nay, beausire; this is no child's play," he said. "I care naught for this girl. I stand as champion for the king against yon traitor Atheling; and if the maiden's cause is his, why then against her too. This is a man's quarrel."

Young Robert would have spoken yet again as his face flushed hot with anger at the knight's con-

temptuous words.　But a firm hand was laid upon
his shoulder, and a strong voice said :

"Then is it mine, Sir Ordgar.　If between man
and man, then will I, with the gracious permission
of our lord the king, stand as champion for this
maiden here and for my good lord, the noble
Atheling, whose liegeman and whose man am I,
next to you, lord king."　And, taking the mate to
the glove which the Princess Edith had flung down
in defiance, he thrust it into the guard of his cappe-
line, or iron skull-cap, in token that he, Godwine of
Winchester, the father of the boy Robert, was the
young girl's champion.

Three days after, in the tilt-yard of Gloucester
Castle, the wager of battle was fought.　It was no
gay tournament show with streaming banners,
gorgeous lists, gayly dressed ladies, flower-bedecked
balconies, and all the splendid display of a tourney
of the knights, of which you read in the stories of
romance and chivalry.　It was a solemn and sombre
gathering in which all the arrangements suggested
only death and gloom, while the accused waited in
suspense, knowing that halter and fagot were prepared for them should their champion fall.　In
quaint and crabbed Latin the old chronicler, John
of Fordun, tells the story of the fight, for which
there is neither need nor space here.　The glove
of each contestant was flung into the lists by the

judge, and the dispute committed for settlement to the power of God and their own good swords. It is a stirring picture of those days of daring and of might, when force took the place of justice, and the deadliest blows were the only convincing arguments. But, though supported by the favor of the king and the display of splendid armor, Ordgar's treachery had its just reward. Virtue triumphed, and vice was punished. Even while treacherously endeavoring (after being once disarmed) to stab the brave Godwine with a knife which he had concealed in his boot, the false Sir Ordgar was overcome, confessed the falsehood of his charge against Edgar the Atheling and Edith his niece, and, as the quaint old record has it, " The strength of his grief and the multitude of his wounds drove out his impious soul."

So young Edith was saved ; and, as is usually the case with men of his character, the Red King's humor changed completely. The victorious Godwine received the arms and lands of the dead Ordgar ; Edgar the Atheling was raised high in trust and honor ; the throne of Scotland, wrested from the Red Donald, was placed once more in the family of King Malcolm, and King William Rufus himself became the guardian and protector of the Princess Edith.

And when, one fatal August day, the Red King

was found pierced by an arrow under the trees of
the New Forest, his younger brother, Duke Henry,
whom men called Beauclerc, " the good scholar,"
for his love of learning and of books, ascended the
throne of England as King Henry I. And the
very year of his accession, on the 11th of Novem-
ber, 1100, he married, in the Abbey of Westminster,
the Princess Edith of Scotland, then a fair young
lady of scarce twenty-one. At the request of her
husband she took, upon her coronation day, the
Norman name of Matilda, or Maud, and by this
name she is known in history and among the
queens of England.

So scarce four and thirty years after the Norman
conquest, a Saxon princess sat upon the throne
of Norman England, the loving wife of the son of
the very man by whom Saxon England was conquered.

" Never, since the battle of Hastings," says Sir
Francis Palgrave, the historian, " had there been
such a joyous day as when Queen Maud was
crowned." Victors and vanquished, Normans and
Saxons, were united at last, and the name of
" Good Queen Maud " was long an honored memory among the people of England.

And she *was* a good queen. In a time of bitter
tyranny, when the common people were but the
serfs and slaves of the haughty and cruel barons,

this young queen labored to bring in kindlier manners and more gentle ways. Beautiful in face, she was still more lovely in heart and life. Her influence upon her husband, Henry the scholar, was seen in the wise laws he made, and the "Charter of King Henry" is said to have been gained by her intercession. This important paper was the first step toward popular liberty. It led the way to Magna Charta, and finally to our own Declaration of Independence. The boys and girls of America, therefore, in common with those of England, can look back with interest and affection upon the romantic story of "Good Queen Maud," the bravehearted girl who showed herself wise and fearless both in the perilous mist at Edinburgh, and, later still, in the yet greater dangers of "the black lists of Gloucester."

JACQUELINE OF HOLLAND
The Girl of the land of Fogs
A.D. 1417.

COUNT WILLIAM OF HAINAULT, of
Zealand and Friesland, Duke of Bavaria
and Sovereign Lord of Holland, held his
court in the great, straggling castle which he
called his " hunting lodge," near to the German

Ocean, and since known by the name of "The Hague." *

Count William was a gallant and courtly knight, learned in all the ways of chivalry, the model of the younger cavaliers, handsome in person, noble in bearing, the surest lance in the tilting-yard, and the stoutest arm in the foray.

Like "Jephtha, Judge of Israel," of whom the mock-mad Hamlet sang to Polonius, Count William had

> "One fair daughter, and no more,
> The which he loved passing well";

and, truth to tell, this fair young Jacqueline, the little "Lady of Holland," as men called her,— but whom Count William, because of her fearless antics and boyish ways, called "Dame Jacob," *— loved her knightly father with equal fervor.

As she sat, that day, in the great Hall of the Knights in the massive castle at The Hague, she could see, among all the knights and nobles who came from far and near to join in the festivities at Count William's court, not one that approached her father in nobility of bearing or manly strength— not even her husband.

---

* "The Hague" is a contraction of the Dutch *'s Gravenhage*—the *haag*, or "hunting lodge," of the *Graf*, or count.

† *Jacqueline* is the French rendering of the Dutch *Jakobine*—the feminine of *Jakob*, or James.

Her husband? Yes. For this little maid of thirteen had been for eight years the wife of the Dauphin of France, the young Prince John of Touraine, to whom she had been married when she was scarce five years old and he barely nine. Surrounded by all the pomp of an age of glitter and display, these royal children lived in their beautiful castle of Quesnoy, in Flanders,* when they were not, as at the time of our story, residents at the court of the powerful Count William of Holland.

Other young people were there, too,—nobles and pages and little ladies-in-waiting; and there was much of the stately ceremonial and flowery talk that in those days of knighthood clothed alike the fears of cowards and the desires of heroes. For there have always been heroes and cowards in the world.

And so, between all these young folk, there was much boastful talk and much harmless gossip: how the little Lady of Courtrai had used the wrong corner of the towel yesterday; how the fat Duchess of Enkhuysen had violated the laws of all etiquette by placing the wrong number of finger-bowls upon her table on St. Jacob's Day; and how the stout young Hubert of Malsen had scattered the rascal merchants of Dort at their Shrovetide fair.

* Now Northeastern France.

Then uprose the young Lord of Arkell.

" Hold, there ! " he cried hotly. " This Hubert of Malsen is but a craven, sirs, if he doth say the merchants of Dort are rascal cowards. Had they been fairly mated, he had no more dared to put his nose within the gates of Dort than dare one of you here to go down yonder amid Count William's lions ! "

" Have a care, friend Otto," said the little Lady of Holland, with warning finger ; " there is one here, at least, who dareth to go amid the lions— my father, sir."

" I said nothing of him, madam," replied Count Otto. " I did mean these young red hats here, who do no more dare to bait your father's lions than to face the Cods of Dort in fair and equal fight."

At this bold speech there was instant commotion. For the nobles and merchants of Holland, four centuries and a half ago, were at open strife with one another. The nobles saw in the increasing prosperity of the merchants the end of their own feudal power and tyranny. The merchants recognized in the arrogant nobles the only bar to the growth of Holland's commercial enterprise. So each faction had its leaders, its partisans, its badges, and its followers. Many and bloody were the feuds and fights that raged through all those

low-lying lands of Holland, as the nobles, or
" Hooks," as they were called—distinguishable by
their big red hats,—and the merchants, or "Cods,"
with their slouch hats of quiet gray, struggled for
the lead in the state.   And how they *did* hate one
another !

Certain of the younger nobles, however, who
were opposed to the reigning house of Holland, of
which Count William, young Jacqueline's father,
was the head, had espoused the cause of the merchants, seeing in their success greater prosperity
and wealth for Holland.   Among these had been
the young Lord of Arkell, now a sort of half prisoner at Count William's court because of certain
bold attempts to favor the Cods in his own castle
of Arkell.   His defiant words therefore raised a
storm of protests.

" Nay, then, Lord of Arkell," said the Dauphin
John, " you, who prate so loudly, would better
prove your words by some sign of your own valor.
You may have dared fight your lady mother, who
so roundly punished you therefor, but a lion hath
not the tender ways of a woman.   Face *you* the
lions, lord count, and I will warrant me they will
not prove as forbearing as did she."

It was common talk at Count William's court
that the brave Lady of Arkell, mother of the Count
Otto, had made her way, disguised, into the castle

of her son, had herself lowered the drawbridge, admitted her armed retainers, overpowered and driven out her rebellious son ; and that then, relenting, she had appealed to Count William to pardon the lad and to receive him at court as hostage for his own fealty. So this fling of the Dauphin's cut deep.

But before the young Otto could return an angry answer, Jacqueline had interfered.

"Nay, nay, my lord," she said to her husband, the Dauphin ; "'t is not a knightly act thus to impeach the honor of a noble guest."

But now the Lord of Arkell had found his tongue.

"My lord prince," he said, bowing low with stately courtesy, "if, as my lady mother and good Count William would force me, I am to be loyal vassal to you, my lieges here, I should but follow where you dare to lead. Go *you* into the lions' den, lord prince, and I will follow you, though it were into old Hercules' very teeth."

It was a shrewd reply, and covered as good a "double-dare" as ever one boy made to another. Some of the manlier of the young courtiers indeed even dared to applaud. But the Dauphin John was stronger in tongue than in heart.

"*Peste !*" he cried contemptuously. "'T is a fool's answer and a fool's will. And well shall we see now how you will sneak out of it all. See, Lord of Arkell, you who can prate so loudly of Cods and lions : here before all, I dare you to face Count William's lions yourself !"

The young Lord of Arkell was in his rich court suit—a tight-fitting, great-sleeved silk jacket, rich, violet *chausses*, or tights, and pointed shoes. But without a word, with scarce a look toward his challenger, he turned to his nearest neighbor, a brave Zeland lad, afterward noted in Dutch history—Francis von Borselen.

"Lend me your gabardine, friend Franz, will you not ?" he said.

The young von Borselen took from the back of the settle, over which it was flung, his gabardine— the long, loose gray cloak that was a sort of overcoat in those days of queer costume.

"It is here, my Otto," he said.

The Lord of Arkell drew the loose gray cloak over his rich silk suit, and turned toward the door.

"Otto von Arkell lets no one call him fool or coward, lord prince," he said. "What I have dared you all to do, *I* dare do, if you do not. See, now : I will face Count William's lions !"

The Princess Jacqueline sprang up in protest.

"No, no ; you shall not !" she cried. "My lord prince did but jest, as did we all. John," she said, turning appealingly to her young husband, who sat sullen and unmoved, "tell him you meant no such murderous test. My father!" she cried, turning now toward Count William, whose attention had been drawn to the dispute, "the Lord of Arkell is pledged to face your lions!"

Count William of Holland dearly loved pluck and nerve.

"Well, daughter mine," he said, "then will he keep his pledge. Friend Otto is a brave young gallant, else had he never dared raised spear and banner, as he did, against his rightful liege."

"But, my father," persisted the gentle-hearted girl, "spear and banner are not lions' jaws. And surely you may not in honor permit the wilful murder of a hostage."

"Nay, madam, have no fear," the Lord of Arkell said, bending in courteous recognition of her interest; "that which I do of mine own free will is no murder, even should it fail."

And he hastened from the hall.

A raised gallery looked down into the spacious inclosure in which Count William kept the living specimens of his own princely badge of the lion. And here the company gathered to see the sport.

With the gray gabardine drawn but loosely over his silken suit, so that he might, if need be, easily slip from it, Otto von Arkell boldly entered the inclosure.

"Soho, Juno! up, Hercules; hollo, up, Ajax!"
cried Count William, from the balcony. "Here
cometh a right royal playfellow—up, up, my beau-
ties!" and the great brutes, roused by the voice of
their master, pulled themselves up, shook themselves awake, and stared at the intruder.

Boldly and without hesitation, while all the
watchers had eyes but for him alone, the young
Lord of Arkell walked straight up to Hercules, the
largest of the three, and laid his hand caressingly
upon the shaggy mane. Close to his side pressed
Juno, the lioness, and, so says the record of the old
Dutch chronicler, von Hildegaersberch, "the lions
did him no harm; he played with them as if they
had been dogs."

But Ajax, fiercest of the three, took no notice of
the lad. Straight across his comrades he looked to
where, scarce a rod behind the daring lad, came
another figure, a light and graceful form in clinging
robes of blue and undergown of cloth of gold—the
Princess Jacqueline herself!

The watchers in the gallery followed the lion's
stare, and saw, with horror, the advancing figure of
this fair young girl. A cry of terror broke from
every lip. The Dauphin John turned pale with
fright, and Count William of Holland, calling out,
"Down, Ajax! back, girl, back!" sprang to his feet
as if he would have vaulted over the gallery rail.

But before he could act, Ajax himself had acted.
With a bound he cleared the intervening space and
crouched at the feet of the fair young Princess
Jacqueline !

The lions must have been in remarkably good
humor on that day, for, as the records tell us, they
did no harm to their visitors. Ajax slowly rose
and looked up into the girl's calm face. Then the
voice of Jacqueline rang out fresh and clear as,
standing with her hand buried in the lion's tawny
mane, she raised her face to the startled galleries.

" You who could dare and yet dared not to do ! "
she cried, " it shall not be said that in all Count
William's court none save the rebel Lord of Arkell
dared to face Count William's lions ! "

The Lord of Arkell sprang to his comrade's side.
With a hurried word of praise he flung the gabardine about her, grasped her arm, and bade her
keep her eyes firmly fixed upon the lions ; then, step
by step, those two foolhardy young persons backed
slowly out of the danger into which they had so
thoughtlessly and unnecessarily forced themselves.

The lions' gate closed behind them with a clang ;
the shouts of approval and of welcome sounded
from the thronging gallery, and over all they heard
the voice of the Lord of Holland mingling com-
mendation and praise with censure for the rashness
of their action.

And it *was* a rash and foolish act.   But we must remember that those were days when such feats were esteemed as brave and valorous.   For the Princess Jaqueline of Holland was reared in the school of so-called chivalry and romance, which in her time was fast approaching its end.   She was, indeed, as one historian declares, the last heroine of knighthood.   Her very titles suggest the days of chivalry. She was Daughter of Holland, Countess of Ponthieu, Duchess of Berry, Lady of Crevecœur, of Montague and Arlœux.   Brought up in the midst of tilts and tournaments, of banquets and feasting, and all the lavish display of the rich Bavarian court, she was, as we learn from her chroniclers, the leader of adoring knights and vassals, the idol of her parents, the ruler of her soft-hearted boy husband, an expert falconer, a daring horsewoman, and a fearless descendant of those woman warriors of her race, Margaret the Empress, and Philippa the Queen, and of a house that traced its descent through the warlike Hohenstaufens back to Charlemagne himself.

All girls admire bravery, even though not themselves personally courageous.   It is not, therefore, surprising that this intrepid and romance-reared young princess, the wife of a lad for whom she never especially cared, and whose society had for political reasons been forced upon her, should have placed as

AJAX SLOWLY ROSE AND LOOKED UP INTO THE GIRL'S CALM FACE.

the hero of her admiration, next to her own fearless father, not the Dauphin John of France, but this brave young rebel lad, Otto, the Lord of Arkell.

But the joyous days of fête and pleasure at Quesnoy, at Paris, and The Hague were fast drawing to a close. On the fourth of April, 1417, the Dauphin John died by poisoning, in his father's castle at Compiègne—the victim of those terrible and relentless feuds that were then disgracing and endangering the feeble throne of France.

The dream of future power and greatness as Queen of France, in which the girl wife of the Dauphin had often indulged, was thus rudely dispelled, and Jacqueline returned to her father's court in Holland, no longer crown princess and heiress to a throne, but simply "Lady of Holland."

But in Holland, too, sorrow was in store for her. Swiftly following the loss of her husband, the Dauphin, came the still heavier blow of her father's death. On the thirtieth of May, 1417, Count William died in his castle of Bouchain, in Hainault, and his sorrowing daughter Jacqueline, now a beautiful girl of sixteen, succeeded to his titles and lordship as Countess and Lady Supreme of Hainault, of Holland, and of Zealand.

For years, however, there had been throughout the Low Countries a strong objection to the rule of a woman. The death of Count William showed the

Cods a way toward greater liberty. Rebellion followed rebellion, and the rule of the Countess Jacqueline was by no means a restful one.

And chief among the rebellious spirits, as leader and counsellor among the Cods, appeared the brave lad who had once been the companion of the prin ess in danger, the young Lord of Arkell.

It was he who lifted the standard of revolt against her regency. Placing the welfare of Holland above personal friendship, and sinking, in his desire for glory, even the chivalry of that day, which should have prompted him to aid rather than annoy this beautiful girl, he raised a considerable army among the knights of the Cods, or liberal party, and the warlike merchants of the cities, took possession of many strong positions in Holland, and occupied, among other places, the important town of Gorkum on the Maas. The stout citadel of the town, was, however, garrisoned with loyal troops. This the Lord of Arkell beseiged, and, demanding its surrender, sent also a haughty challenge to the young countess, who was hastening to the relief of her beleaguered town.

Jacqueline's answer was swift and unmistakable. With three hundred ships and six thousand knights and men-at-arms, she sailed from the old harbor of Rotterdam, and the lion-flag of her house soon floated above the loyal citadel of Gorkum.

Her doughty Dutch general, von Brederode, counselled immediate attack, but the girl countess, though full of enthusiasm and determination, hesitated.

From her station in the citadel she looked over the scene before her. Here, along the low bank of the river Maas, stretched the camp of her own followers, and the little gayly colored boats that had brought her army up the river from the red roofs of Rotterdam. There, stretching out into the flat country beyond the straggling streets of Gorkum, lay the tents of the rebels. And yet they were all her countrymen—rebels and retainers alike. Hollanders all, they were ever ready to combine for the defence of their homeland when threatened by foreign foes or by the destroying ocean floods.

Jacqueline's eye caught the flutter of the broad banner of the house of Arkell that waved over the rebel camp.

Again she saw the brave lad who alone of all her father's court, save she, had dared to face Count William's lions ; again the remembrance of how his daring had made him one of her heroes, filled her heart, and a dream of what might be possessed her. Her boy husband, the French Dauphin, was dead, and she was pledged by her dying father's command to marry her cousin, whom she detested, Duke John of Brabant. But how much better, so she reasoned, that the name and might of her house as rulers of Holland should be upheld by a brave and fearless knight. On the impulse of this thought she summoned a loyal and trusted vassal to her aid.

"Von Leyenburg," she said, "go you in haste and in secret to the Lord of Arkell, and bear from me this message for his ear alone. Thus says the Lady of Holland : ' Were it not better, Otto of Arkell, that we join hands in marriage before the altar, than that we spill the blood of faithful followers and vassals in a cruel fight ?' "

It was a singular, and perhaps, to our modern ears, a most unladylike proposal ; but it shows how, even in the heart of a sovereign countess and a girl general, warlike desires may give place to gentler thoughts.

To the Lord Arkell, however, this unexpected proposition came as an indication of weakness.

" My lady countess fears to face my determined followers," he thought. " Let me but force this fight and the victory is mine. In that is greater glory and more of power than being husband to the Lady of Holland."

And so he returned a most ungracious answer :

"Tell the Countess Jacqueline," he said to the knight of Leyenburg, "that the honor of her hand I cannot accept. I am her foe, and would rather die than marry her."

All the hot blood of her ancestors flamed in wrath as young Jacqueline heard this reply of the rebel lord.

"Crush we these rebel curs, von Brederode," she cried, pointing to the banner of Arkell; "for by my father's memory, they shall have neither mercy nor life from me."

Fast upon the curt refusal of the Lord of Arkell came his message of defiance.

"Hear ye, Countess of Holland," rang out the challenge of the herald of Arkell, as his trumpet-blast sounded before the gate of the citadel, "the free Lord of Arkell here giveth you word and warning that he will fight against you on the morrow!"

And from the citadel came back this ringing reply, as the knight of Leyenburg made answer for his sovereign lady :

"Hear ye, sir Herald, and answer thus to the rebel Lord of Arkell : 'For the purpose of fighting him came we here, and fight him we will, until he and his rebels are beaten and dead.' Long live our Sovereign Lady of Holland !"

On the morrow, a murky December day, in the year 1417, the battle was joined, as announced. On the low plain beyond the city, knights and men-at-arms, archers and spearmen, closed in the shock of battle, and a stubborn and bloody fight it was.

Seven times did the knights of Jacqueline, glit-tering in their steel armor, clash into the rebel ranks; seven times were they driven back, until, at last, the Lord of Arkell, with a fiery charge, forced them against the very gates of the citadel. The brave von Brederode fell pierced with wounds, and the day seemed lost, indeed, to the Lady of Holland.

Then Jacqueline the Countess, seeing her cause in danger—like another Joan of Arc, though she was indeed a younger and much more beautiful girl general,—seized the lion-banner of her house, and, at the head of her reserve troops, charged through the open gate straight into the ranks of her vic-torious foes. There was neither mercy nor gentle-ness in her heart then. As when she had cowed with a look Ajax, the lion, so now, with defiance and wrath in her face, she dashed straight at the foe.

Her disheartened knights rallied around her, and, following the impetuous girl, they wielded axe and lance for the final struggle. The result came quickly. The ponderous battle-axe of the knight of Leyenburg crashed through the helmet of the Lord of Arkell, and as the brave young leader fell to the ground, his panic-stricken fol-lowers turned and fled. The troops of Jacqueline pursued them through the streets of Gorkum and out into the open country, and the vengeance of the countess was sharp and merciless.

But in the flush of victory wrath gave way to pity again, and the young conqueror is reported to have said, sadly and in tears :

"Ah ! I have won, and yet how have I lost !"

But the knights and nobles who followed her banner loudly praised her valor and her fearlessness, and their highest and most knightly vow thereafter was to swear " By the courage of our Princess."

The brilliant victory of this girl of sixteen was not, however, to accomplish her desires. Peace never came to her. Harassed by rebellion at home, and persecuted by her relentless and perfidious uncles, Count John of Bavaria, rightly called " the Pitiless," and Duke Philip of Burgundy, falsely called " the Good," she, who had once been Crown Princess of France and Lady of Holland, died at the early age of thirty-six, stripped of all her titles and estates. It is, however, pleasant to think that she was happy in the love of her husband, the baron of the forests of the Duke of Burgundy, a plain Dutch gentleman, Francis von Borselen, the lad who, years before, had furnished the gray gabardine that had shielded Count William's daughter from her father's lions.

The story of Jacqueline of Holland is one of the

most romantic that has come down to us from those romantic days of the knights. Happy only in her earliest and latest years, she is, nevertheless, a bright and attractive figure against the dark background of feudal tyranny and crime. The story of her womanhood should indeed be told, if we would study her life as a whole ; but for us, who can in this paper deal only with her romantic girlhood, her young life is to be taken as a type of the stirring and extravagant days of chivalry.

And we cannot but think with sadness upon the power for good that she might have been in her land of fogs and floods if, instead of being made the tool of party hate and the ambitions of men, her frank and fearless girl nature had been trained to gentle ways and charitable deeds.

To be " the most picturesque figure in the history of Holland," as she has been called, is distinction indeed ; but higher still must surely be that gentleness of character and nobility of soul that, in these days of ours, may be acquired by every girl and boy who reads this romantic story of the Countess Jacqueline, the fair young Lady of Holland.

CATARINA OF VENICE:

THE GIRL OF THE GRAND CANAL.

[Afterward known as Queen of Cyprus and " Daughter of the Republic."]
A.D. 1466.

" WHO is he? Why, do you not know, Catarina *mia ?* 'T is his Most Puissant Excellency, the mighty Lord of Lusignan, the runaway Heir of Jerusalem, the beggar Prince of Cyprus, with more titles to his name—ho, ho, ho !—than he hath jackets to his back; and with more dodging than ducats, so 't is said, when the time to pay for his lodging draweth nigh. Holo, Messer Principino ! Give you good-day, Lord of Lusignan ! Ho, below there ! here is tribute for you !"

And down upon the head of a certain sad-faced, seedy-looking young fellow in the piazza, or square, beneath, descended a rattling shower of bonbons, thrown by the hand of the speaker, a brown-faced Venetian lad of sixteen.

But little Catarina Cornaro, just freed from the imprisonment of her convent-school at Padua, felt her heart go out in pity towards this homeless young prince, who just now seemed to be the butt for all the riot and teasing of the boys of the Great Republic.

" Nay, nay, my Giorgio," she said to her brother; " 't is neither fair nor wise so to beset one in dire distress. The good sisters of our school have often told us that 't is better to be a beggar than a dullard; and sure yon prince, as you do say he is, looketh to be no dolt. But ah, see there!" she cried, leaning far over the gayly draped balcony; "see, he can well use his fists, can he not! Nay, though, 't is a shame so to beset him, say I. Why should our lads so misuse a stranger and a prince?"

It was the Feast Day of St. Mark, one of the jolliest of the old-time holidays of Venice, that wonderful City of the Sea, whose patron and guardian St. Mark, the apostle, was supposed to be. Gondolas, rich with draperies of every hue that completely concealed their frames of sombre black, shot in and out, and up and down all the water-

streets of the beautiful city ; while towering palace
and humbler dwelling alike were gay with gorgeous
hangings and fluttering streamers.

In noticeable contrast with all the brilliant costumes and laughing faces around him was the lad
who just now seemed in so dire a strait. He had
paused to watch one of the passing pageants from
the steps of the Palazzo Cornaro, quite near the spot
where, a century later, the famous bridge known as
the Rialto spanned the Street of the Nobles, or
Grand Canal—one of the most notable spots in
the history of Venice the Wonderful.

The lad was indeed a prince, the representative
of a lordly house that for more than five hundred
years had been strong and powerful, first as barons
of France, and later as rulers of the Crusaders'
kingdom of Jerusalem and the barbaric but wealthy
island of Cyprus.   But poor Giacomo, or James, of
Lusignan, royal prince though he was, had been
banished from his father's court in Cyprus.   He had
dared rebel against the authority of his step-mother,
a cruel Greek princess from Constantinople, who
ruled her feeble old husband and persecuted her
spirited young step-son, the Prince Giacomo.

And so, with neither money nor friends to help
him on, he had wandered to Venice. But Venice
in 1466, a rich, proud, and prosperous city, was a
very poor place for a lad who had neither friends

nor money; for, of course, the royal prince of a
little island in the Mediterranean could not so de-
mean himself as to soil his hands with work!

So I imagine that young Prince Giacomo had any
thing but a pleasant time in Venice. On this
particular Feast Day of St. Mark, I am certain that
he was having the most unpleasant of all his bitter
experiences, as, backed up against one of the columns
of the Cornaro Palace, he found himself surrounded
by a crowd of thoughtless young Venetians, who
were teasing and bullying him to the full content of
their brutal young hearts.

The Italian temper is known to be both hot and
hasty; but the temper of oriental Cyprus is even
more fiery, and so it was not surprising that, in this
most one-sided fray, the fun soon became fighting
in earnest; for anger begets anger.

All about the young prince was a tossing throng
of restless and angry boys, while the beleaguered
lad, still standing at bay, flourished a wicked-looking
stiletto above his head and answered taunt with
taunt.

At this instant the door of the Cornaro Palace
opened quickly, and the Prince Giacomo felt himself drawn bodily within; while a bright-faced young
girl with flashing eye and defiant air confronted his
greatly surprised tormentors.

"Shame, shame upon you, boys of Venice," she

cried, " thus to ill-use a stranger in your town ! Is
a score of such as you against one poor lad the
boasted chivalry of Venice ? *Eh via !* the very
fisher-lads of Mendicoli could teach you better
ways ! "

Taken quite aback by this sudden apparition and
these stinging words, the boys dispersed with scarce
an attempt to reply, and all the more hastily because
they spied, coming up the Grand Canal, the gorgeous gondola of the Companions of the Stocking,
an association of young men under whose charge
and supervision all the pageants and displays of old
Venice were given.

So the piazza was speedily cleared ; and the
Prince Giacomo, with many words of thanks to his
young and unknown deliverers, hurried from the
spot which had so nearly proved disastrous to him.

Changes came suddenly in those unsettled times.
Within two years both the Greek step-mother and
the feeble old king were dead, and Prince Giacomo,
after a struggle for supremacy with his half-sister
Carlotta, became King of Cyprus.

Now Cyprus, though scarcely as large as the
State of Connecticut, was a very desirable possession, and one that Venice greatly coveted. Some
of her citizens owned land there, and among these
was Marco Cornaro, father of Catarina. And so
it happened that, soon after the accession of King

Giacomo, Messer Andrea Cornaro, the uncle of Catarina, came to Cyprus to inspect and improve the lands belonging to his brother Marco.

Venice, in those days was so great a power that the Venetian merchants were highly esteemed in all the courts of Europe. And Uncle Andrea, who had probably loaned the new king of Cyprus a goodly store of Venetian ducats, became quite friendly with the young monarch, and gave him much sage advice.

One day—it seemed as if purely by accident, but those old Venetians were both shrewd and far-seeing—Uncle Andrea, talking of the glories of Venice, showed to King Giacomo a picture of his niece, Catarina Cornaro, then a beautiful girl of fourteen.

King Giacomo came of a house that was quick to form friendships and antipathies, loves and hates. He " fell violently in love with the picture,"—so the story goes,—and expressed to Andrea Cornaro his desire to see and know the original.

" That face seemeth strangely familiar, Messer Cornaro," he said.

He held the portrait in his hands, and seemed struggling with an uncertain memory. Suddenly his face lighted up, and he exclaimed joyfully :

" So ; I have it ! Messer Cornaro, I know your niece,"

"You know her, sire?" echoed the surprised Uncle Andrea.

"Ay, that indeed I do," said the king. "This is the same fair and brave young maiden who delivered me from a rascal rout of boys on the Grand Canal at Venice, on St. Mark's Day, scarce two years ago." And King Giacomo smiled and bowed at the picture as if it were the living Catarina instead of her simple portrait.

Here now was news for Uncle Andrea. And you may be sure he was too good a Venetian and too loyal a Cornaro not to turn it to the best advantage. So he stimulated the young king's evident inclination as cunningly as he was able. His niece Catarina, he assured the king, was as good as she was beautiful, and as clever as she was both.

"But then," he declared, "Venice hath many fair daughters, sire, whom the king's choice would honor, and Catarina is but a young maid yet. Would it not be wiser, when you choose a queen, to select some older *donzella* for your bride? Though it will, I can aver, be hard to choose a fairer."

It is just such half-way opposition that renders a nature like that of this young monarch all the more determined. No! King Giacomo would have Catarina, and Catarina only, for his bride and queen. Messer Cornaro must secure her for him.

But shrewd Uncle Andrea still feared the jealousy of his fellow-Venetians. Why should the house of Cornaro, they would demand, be so openly preferred? And so, at his suggestion, an ambassador was despatched to Venice soliciting an alliance with the Great Republic, and asking from the senate the hand of some high-born maid of Venice in marriage for his highness, the King of Cyprus. But you may be very sure that the ambassador had special and secret instructions alike from King Giacomo and from Uncle Andrea just how and whom to choose.

The ambassador came to Venice, and soon the senate issued its commands that upon a certain day the noblest and fairest of the daughters of Venice —one from each of the patrician families—should appear in the great Council Hall of the Ducal Palace in order that the ambassador of the King of Cyprus might select a fitting bride for his royal master. It reads quite like one of the old fairy stories, does it not? Only in this case the dragon who was to take away the fairest maiden as his tribute was no monster, but the brave young king of a lovely island realm.

The Palace of the Doges—the Palazzo Ducale of old Venice—is familiar to all who have ever seen a picture of the Square of St. Mark's, the best known spot in that famous City of the Sea. It is the low,

rectangular, richly decorated building with its long
row of columns and arcades that stand out so
prominently in photograph and engraving.   It
has seen many a splendid pageant, but it never witnessed a fairer sight than when on a certain bright
day of the year 1468 seventy-two of the daughters
of Venice, gorgeous in the rich costumes of that
most lavish city of a lavish age, gathered in the
great *Consiglio*, or Council Hall.

Up the *Scala d'Oro*, or Golden Staircase, built
only for the use of the nobles, they came, escorted
by the ducal guards, gleaming in their richest uni-
forms.   The great Council Hall was one mass of
color ; the splendid dresses of the ladies, the scarlet
robes of the senators and high officials of the Republic, the imposing vestments of the old doge,
Cristofero Moro, as he sat in state upon his massive throne, and the bewildering array of the seventy-two candidates for a king's choice.   Seventy-
two, I say, but in all that company of puffed and
powdered, coifed and combed young ladies, standing
tall and uncomfortable on their ridiculously high-
heeled shoes, one alone was simply dressed and ap-
parently unaffected by the gorgeousness of her companions, the seventy-second and youngest of them all.

She was a girl of fourteen.   Face and form were
equally beautiful, and a mass of " dark gold hair "
crowned her " queenly head."   While the other girls

appeared nervous or anxious, she seemed uncon-
cerned, and her face wore even a peculiar little
smile, as if she were contrasting the poor badgered
young prince of St. Mark's Day with the present
King of Cyprus hunting for a bride. "*Eh via !*"
she said to herself, "'t is almost as if it were a revenge upon us for our former churlishness, that he
thus now puts us to shame."

The ambassador of Cyprus, swarthy of face and
stately in bearing, entered the great hall. With
him came his attendant retinue of Cypriote nobles.
Kneeling before the doge, the ambassador presented
the petition of his master, the King of Cyprus,
seeking alliance and friendship with Venice.

"And the better to secure this and the more
firmly to cement it, Eccellenza," said the ambassador, "my lord and master the king doth crave from
your puissant state the hand of some high-born
damsel of the Republic as that of his loving and
acknowledged queen."

The old doge waved his hand toward the fair and
anxious seventy-two.

"Behold, noble sir," he said, "the fairest and
noblest of our maidens of Venice. Let your eye
seek among these a fitting bride for your lord, the
King of Cyprus, and it shall be our pleasure to give
her to him in such a manner as shall suit the power
and dignity of the State of Venice."

Courteous and stately still, but with a shrewd and critical eye, the ambassador of Cyprus slowly passed from candidate to candidate, with here a pleasant word and there a look of admiration; to this one a honeyed compliment upon her beauty, to that one a bit of praise for her elegance of dress.

How oddly this all sounds to us with our modern ideas of propriety and good taste! It seems a sort of Prize Girl Show, does it not? Or, it is like a competitive examination for a royal bride.

But, like too many such examinations, this one had already been settled beforehand. The King had decided to whom the prize of his crown should go, and so, at the proper time, the critical ambassador stopped before a slight girl of fourteen, dressed in a robe of simple white.

"*Donzella mia,*" he said courteously, but in a low tone; "are not you the daughter of Messer Marco Cornaro, the noble merchant of the Via Merceria?"

"I am, my lord," the girl replied.

"My royal master greets you through me," he said. "He recalls the day when you did give him shelter, and he invites you to share with him the throne of Cyprus. Shall this be as he wishes?"

And the girl, with a deep courtesy in acknowledgment of the stately obeisance of the ambassador, said simply, "That shall be, my lord, as my father and his Excellency shall say."

The ambassador of Cyprus took the young girl's hand, and, conducting her through all that splendid company, presented her before the doge's throne.

"Excellency," he said, "Cyprus hath made her choice. We present to you, if so it shall please your grace, our future queen, this fair young maid, Catarina, the daughter of the noble Marco Cornaro, merchant and senator of the Republic."

What the seventy-one disappointed young ladies thought of the King's choice, or what they said about it when they were safely at home once more, history does not record. But history does record the splendors and display of the ceremonial with which the gray-haired old doge, Cristofero Moro, in the great hall of the palace, surrounded by the senators of the Republic and all the rank and power of the State of Venice, formally adopted Catarina as a "daughter of the Republic." Thus to the dignity of her father's house was added the majesty of the great Republic. Her marriage portion was placed at one hundred thousand ducats, and Cyprus was granted, on behalf of this "daughter of the Republic," the alliance and protection of Venice.

The ambassador of Cyprus standing before the altar of St. Mark's as the personal representative of his master, King Giacomo was married "by proxy" to the young Venetian girl; while the doge, representing her new father, the republic, gave her

away in marriage, and Catarina Cornaro, amid the
blessings of the priests, the shouts of the people,
and the demonstrations of clashing music and wav-
ing banners, was solemnly proclaimed Queen of
Cyprus, of Jerusalem, and of Armenia.

But the gorgeous display, before which even the
fabled wonders of the "Arabian Nights" were but
poor affairs, did not conclude here. Following the
splendors of the marriage ceremony and the wed-
ding-feast, came the pageant of departure. The
Grand Canal was ablaze with gorgeous colors and
decorations. The broad water-steps of the Piazza
of St. Mark was soft with carpets of tapestry,
and at the foot of the stairs floated the most
beautiful boat in the world, the *Bucentaur* or
state gondola, of Venice. Its high, carved prow
and framework were one mass of golden decorations. White statues of the saints, carved heads of
the lion of St. Mark, the doge's cap, and the emblems of the Republic adorned it throughout. Silken
streamers of blue and scarlet floated from its standards ; and its sides were draped in velvet hangings
of crimson and royal purple. The long oars were
scarlet and gold, and the rowers were resplenden
in suits of blue and silver. A great velvet-covered
throne stood on the upper deck, and at its right was
a chair of state, glistening with gold.

Down the tapestried stairway came the Doge of

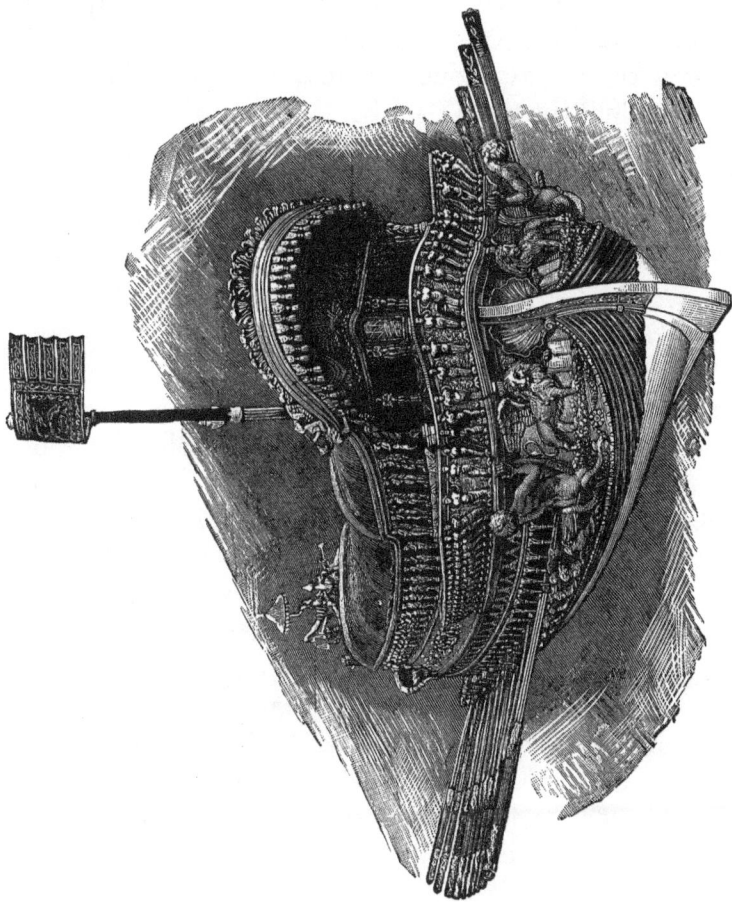

THE BUCENTAUR, OR STATE BARGE OF VENICE.

Venice, and, resting upon his arm, in a white bridal
dress covered with pearls, walked the girl queen
Catarina.   Doge and daughter seated themselves
upon their sumptuous thrones, their glittering retinue filled the beautiful boat, the scarlet oars dipped into the water ; and then, with music playing,
banners streaming, and a grand escort of boats of
every conceivable shape, flashing in decoration and
gorgeous in mingled colors, the bridal train floated
down the Grand Canal, on past the outlying islands,
and between the great fortresses to where, upon
the broad Adriatic, the galleys were waiting to take
the new Queen to her island kingdom off the shores
of Greece.   And there, in his queer old town of
Famagusta, built with a curious commingling of
Saracen, Grecian, and Norman ideas, King Giacomo
met his bride.

So they were married, and for five happy years
all went well with the young King and Queen.
Then came troubles.   King Giacomo died suddenly
from a cold caught while hunting, so it was said ;
though some averred that he had been poisoned,
either by his half-sister Carlotta, with whom he had
contended for his throne, or by some mercenary of
Venice, who desired his realm for that voracious
Republic.

But if this latter was the case, the voracious Republic of Venice was not to find an easy prey.   The

THE BUCENTAUR BEARING THE QUEEN CATERINA AND THE BRIDAL TRAIN.

young Queen Catarina proclaimed her baby boy King of Cyprus, and defied the Great Republic. Venice, surprised at this rebellion of its adopted " daughter," dispatched embassy after embassy to demand submission.   But the young mother was brave and stood boldly up for the rights of her son.

But he, too, died.   Then Catarina, true to the memory of her husband and her boy, strove to re· tain the throne intact.   For years she ruled as Queen of Cyprus, despite the threatenings of her home Republic and the conspiracies of her ene- mies.   Her one answer to the demands of Venice was :

" Tell the Republic I have determined never to remarry.   When I am dead, the throne of Cyprus shall go to the State, my heir.   But until that day I am Queen of Cyprus ! "

Then her brother Giorgio, the same who in ear- lier days had looked down with her from the Cor- naro Palace upon the outcast Prince of Cyprus, came to her as ambassador of the Republic.   His entreaties and his assurance that, unless she com- plied with the senate's demand, the protection of Venice would be withdrawn, and the island kingdom left a prey to Saracen pirates and African robbers, at last carried the day.   Worn out with long con- tending, fearful, not for herself but for her subjects

of Cyprus,— she yielded to the demands of the
senate, and abdicated in favor of the Republic.

Then she returned to Venice. The same wealth
of display and ceremonial that had attended her
departure welcomed the return of this obedient
daughter of the Republic, now no longer a light-
hearted young girl, but a dethroned queen, a
widowed and childless woman.

She was allowed to retain her royal title of
Queen of Cypus, and a noble domain was given
her for a home in the town of Asola, up among the
northern mountains. Here, in a massive castle,
she held her court. It was a bright and happy
company, the home of poetry and music, the arts,
and all the culture and refinement of that age, when
learning belonged to the few and the people were
sunk in densest ignorance.

Here Titian, the great artist, painted the portrait of the exiled queen that has come down to
us. Here she lived for years, sad in her memories
of the past, but happy in her helpfulness of others
until, on her way to visit her brother Giorgio in
Venice, she was stricken with a sudden fever, and
died in the palace in which she had played as a child.

With pomp and display, as was the wont of the
Great Republic, with a city hung with emblems of
mourning, and with the solemn strains of dirge and
mass filling the air, out from the great hall of the

Palazzo Cornaro, on, across the heavily draped
bridge that spanned the Grand Canal from the
water-gate of the palace, along the broad piazza
crowded with a silent throng, and into the Church
of the Holy Apostles, the funeral procession slowly
passed.   The service closed, and in the great Cornaro tomb in the family chapel, at last was laid to
rest the body of one who had enjoyed much but
suffered more—the sorrowful Queen of Cyprus, the
once bright and beautiful " Daughter of the Republic."

Venice to-day is mouldy and wasting.   The
palace in which Catarina Cornaro spent her girlhood is now a pawnbroker's shop.   The last living
representative of the haughty house of Lusignan—
Kings, in their day, of Cyprus, of Jerusalem, and
of Armenia—is said to be a waiter in a French café.
So royalty withers and power fades.   There is no
title to nobility save character, and no family pride
so unfading as a spotless name.   But, though palace
and family have both decayed, the beautiful girl
who was once the glory of Venice and whom great
artists loved to paint, sends us across the ages, in a
flash of regal splendor, a lesson of loyalty and helpfulness.   This, indeed, will outlive all their queenly
titles, and shows her to us as the bright-hearted girl
who, in spite of sorrow, of trouble, and of loss, de-
veloped into the strong and self-reliant woman.

THERESA OF AVILA:

THE GIRL OF THE SPANISH SIERRAS.

[Afterward known as St. Theresa of Avila.]
A.D. 1525.

IT is a stern and gray old city that the sun looks down upon, when once he does show his jolly face above the saw-like ridges of the grim Guadarrama Mountains in Central Spain; a stern and gray old city as well it may be, for it is one of the very old towns of Western Europe—Avila, said by some to have been built by Albula, the mother of Hercules nearly four thousand years ago.

Whether or not it was the place in which that baby gymnast strangled the serpents who sought to kill him in his cradle, it is indeed ancient enough to suit any boy or girl who likes to dig among the relics of the past. For more than eight centuries the same granite walls that now surround it have lifted their gray ramparts out of the vast and granite-covered plains that make the country so wild and lonesome, while its eighty-six towers and gateways, still unbroken and complete, tell of its strength and importance in those far-off days, when the Cross was battling with the Crescent, and Christian Spain, step by step, was forcing Mohammedan Spain back to the blue Mediterranean and the arid wastes of Africa, from which, centuries before, the followers of the Arabian Prophet had come.

At the time of our story, in the year 1525, this forcing process was about over. Under the relentless measures of Ferdinand and Isabella, with whose story all American children, at least, should be familiar, the last Moorish stronghold had fallen, in the very year in which Columbus discovered America, and Spain, from the Pyrenees to the Straits of Gibraltar, acknowledged the mastership of its Christian sovereigns.

But the centuries of warfare that had made the Spaniards a fierce and warlike race, had also filled Spain with frowning castles and embattled towns. And such an embattled town was this same city of Avila, in which, in 1525, lived the stern and pious old grandee, Don Alphonso Sanchez de Cepeda, his sentimental and romance-loving wife, the Donna Beatrix, and their twelve sturdy and healthy children.

Religious warfare, as it is the most bitter and relentless of strifes, is also the most brutal. It turns the natures of men and women into quite a

"SO, RUNAWAYS, WE HAVE FOUND YOU," CRIED BROTHER IAGO.

different channel from the one in which the truths they are fighting for would seek to lead them ; and of all relentless and brutal religious wars, few have been more bitter than the one that for fully five hundred years had wasted the land of Spain.

To battle for the Cross, to gain renown in fights against the Infidels—as the Moors were then called, —to " obtain martyrdom " among the followers of Mohammed—these were reckoned by the Christians of crusading days as the highest honor that life could bring or death bestow. It is no wonder, therefore, that in a family, the father of which had been himself a fighter of Infidels, and the mother a reader and dreamer of all the romantic stories that such conflicts create, the children also should be full of that spirit of hatred toward a conquered foe that came from so bitter and long-continuing a warfare.

Don Alphonso's religion had little in it of cheer-fulness and love　It was of the stern and pitiless kind that called for sacrifice and penance, and all those uncomfortable and unnecessary forms by which too many good people, even in this more enlightened day, think to ease their troubled con-sciences, or to satisfy the fancied demands of the Good Father, who really requires none of these foolish and most unpleasant self-punishments.

But such a belief was the rule in Don Alphonso's

day, and when it could lay so strong a hold upon
grown men and women, it would, of course, be likely
to work in peculiar ways with thoughtful and conscientious children, who, understanding little of the
real meaning of sacrifice and penance, felt it their
duty to do something as proof of their belief.

So it came about that little ten-year-old Theresa,
one of the numerous girls of the Cepeda family,
thought as deeply of these things as her small mind
was capable. She was of a peculiarly sympathetic,
romantic, and conscientious nature, and she felt it
her duty to do something to show her devotion to
the faith for which her father had fought so valiantly, and which the nuns and priests, who were her
teachers, so vigorously impressed upon her.

She had been taught that alike the punishment
or the glory that must follow her life on earth were
to last forever. Forever ! this was a word that
even a thoughtful little maiden like Theresa could
not comprehend. So she sought her mother.

" Forever ? how long is forever, mother mine ? "
she asked.

But the Donna Beatrix was just then too deeply
interested in the tragic story of the two lovers,
Calixto and Melibea, in the Señor Fernando de
Rojas' tear-compelling story, to be able to enter into
the discussion of so deep a question.

" Forever," she said, looking up from the thick

and crabbed black-letter pages, "why forever is forever, child—always. Pray do not trouble me with such questions; just as I am in the midst of this beautiful death-scene too."

The little girl found she could gain no knowledge from this source, and she feared to question her stern and bigoted old father. So she sought her favorite brother Pedro—a bright little fellow of seven, who adored and thoroughly believed in his sister Theresa.

To Pedro, then, Theresa confided her belief that, if forever was so long a time as "always," it would be most unpleasant to suffer "always," if by any chance they should do any thing wrong. It would be far better, so argued this little logician, to die now and end the problem, than to live and run so great a risk. She told him, too, that, as they knew from their mother's tales, the most beautiful, the most glorious way to die was as a martyr among the infidel Moors. So she proposed to Pedro that she and he should not say a word to any one, but just start off at once as crusaders on their own accounts, and lose their lives but save their souls as martyrs among the Moors.

The suggestion had all the effect of novelty to the little Pedro, and while he did not altogether relish the idea of losing his life among the Moors, still the possibility of a change presented itself with all the attractions that the thought of trying something new always has for children. Besides, he had great respect for his sister's judgment.

"Well, let us be crusaders," he said, "and perhaps we need not be martyrs, sister. I don't think that would be so very pleasant, do you? Who knows; perhaps we may be victorious crusaders and conquer the Infidels just as did Ruy Diaz the Cid.* See here, Theresa; I have my sword and you can take your cross, and we can have such a nice crusade, and may be the infidel Moors will run away from us just as they did from the Cid and leave us their cities and their gold and treasure? Don't you remember what mother read us, how the Cid won Castelon, with its silver and its gold?"

And the little fellow spouted most valiantly this portion of the famous poem of the exploits of the Cid (the *Poema del Cid*), with the martial spirit of which stirring rhyme his romantic mother had filled her children :

"Smite, smite, my knights, for mercy's sake—on boldly to the
   war ;
 I am Ruy Diaz of Bivar, the Cid Campeador !
 Three hundred lances then were couched, with pennons
   streaming gay ;

---

* The Cid was the great hero of Spanish romance. The stories of his valor have been the joy of Spaniards, old and young, for centuries. Cid is a corruption of the Moorish word *seyd* or *said*, and means master.

Three hundred shields were piercéd through—no steel the
　　shock might stay ; —
Three hundred hauberks were torn off in that encounter sore ;
Three hundred snow-white pennons were crimson-dyed in
　　gore ;
Three hundred chargers wandered loose—their lords were
　　overthrown ;
The Christians cry 'St. James for Spain !' the Moormen
　　cry 'Mahoun !'"

Theresa applauded her little brother's eloquent
recitation, and thought him a very smart boy ; but
she said rather sadly : "I fear me it will not be that
way, my Pedro ; for martyrdom means, as mother
has told us, the giving up of our life rather than
bow to the false faith of the Infidel, and thus to save
our souls and have a crown of glory."

"The crown would be very nice, I suppose, sister," said practical young Pedro, "especially if it
was all so fine as the one they say the young King
Carlos * wears—Emperor, too, now, is he not?
Could we be emperors, too, sister, if we were martyrs, and had each a crown ? But we must be crusaders first, I suppose. Come, let us go at once."

The road from granite-walled Avila to the south
is across a wild and desolate waste, frowned down
upon on either hand by the savage crests of the
grim sierras of the Guadarrama. It winds along

* King Charles the Fifth was at this time King of Spain, and had just
been elected Emperor of Germany.

gorges and ravines and rocky river-beds, and has always been, even in the days of Spanish power and glory, about as untamed and savagely picturesque a road as one could well imagine.

Along this hard and desolate road, only a few days after their determination had been reached, to start upon a crusade the brother and sister plodded. Theresa carried her crucifix, and Pedro his toy sword, while in a little wallet at his side were a few bits of food taken from the home larder. This stock of food had, of course, been taken without the knowledge of the mother, who knew nothing of their crusade, and this, therefore, furnished for Theresa another sin, for which she must do penance, and another reason for the desired martyrdom.

They had really only proceeded a few miles into the mountains beyond Avila, but already their sturdy little legs were tired, and their stout little backs were sore. Pedro thought crusading not such very great fun after all ; he was always hungry and thirsty, and Theresa would only let him take a bite once in a while.

" Don't you suppose there is a Moorish castle somewhere around here that we could capture, and so get plenty to eat ?" he inquired of his sister. " That is what the Cid was always finding. Don't you remember how nicely he got into Alcacer and slew eleven Infidel knights, and found ever so much

gold and things to eat?   This is what he said, you
know :

> " ' On, on, my knights, and smite the foe !
>   And falter not, I pray ;
>   For by the grace of God, I trow,
>   The town is ours this day ! ' "

" O Pedro, dear, why will you think so much of
things to eat," groaned Theresa.   " Do you not know
that to be hungry is one way to be a martyr.   And
besides, it is, I doubt not, our just punishment for
having taken any thing to eat without letting mother
know.   We must suffer and be strong, little brother."

"That 's just like a girl," cried Pedro, a trifle
scornfully.   " How can we be strong if we suffer ?
I can't, I know."

But before Theresa could enter upon an explana-
tion of this most difficult problem—one that has
troubled many older heads than little Pedro's,—both
the children started in surprise, and then involun-
tarily shrunk closer to the dark gray rock in whose
shadow they were resting.   For there, not a hundred yards distant, coming around a turn in the
road, was one of the very Infidels they had come
out to meet and conquer, or be martyred by.

He was a rather imposing-looking but not a for-
midable old man.   His cloak or mantle of brown
stuff was worn and ragged, his turban was quite as
dingy, but the long white beard that fell upon his

breast made his swarthy face look even fiercer than it really was, and the stout staff, with which he helped himself over the uneven road, seemed to the little crusaders some terrible weapon of torture and of martyrdom.

But Pedro was a valiant little fellow after all. The fighting spirit of his father the Don burned within him, and few little folks of seven know what caution is. He whispered to his sister, whose hand he had at first clutched in terror, a word of assurance.

"Be not afraid, sister mine," he said. "Yonder comes the Infidel we have gone forth to find. Do you suppose he has a whole great army following him? Hold up your crucifix, and I will strike him with my sword. The castle can't be far away, and perhaps we can conquer this old Infidel and find a good dinner in his castle. That's just what the Cid would have done. You know what he said:

> "'Far from our land, far from Castile
> We here are banishéd;
> If with the Moors we battle not,
> I wot we get no bread.'

Let us battle with him at once."

And before his sister with restraining hand, could hold him back the plucky young crusader flourished his sword furiously and charged down upon the old Moor, who now in turn started in sur-

prise and drew aside from the path of the determined little warrior.

> " Now yield thee, yield thee, pagan prince,
>   Or die in crimson gore ;
>   I am Ruy Diaz of Bivar,
>   The Cid Campeador ! "

shouted the little crusader, charging against his
pagan enemy at a furious rate.

"O spare him, spare my brother, noble emir.
Let me die in his stead," cried the terrified Theresa,
not quite so confident now as to the pleasure of
martyrdom.

The old man stretched out his staff and stopped
the headlong dash of the boy. Then laying a hand
lightly on his assailant's head he looked smilingly
toward Theresa.

" Neither prince nor emir am I, Christian maiden,"
he said, " but the poor Morisco Abd-el-'Aman of Cordova, seeking my son Ali, who, men say, is servant
to a family in Valladolid. Pray you if you have
aught to eat give some to me, for I am famishing."

This was not exactly martyrdom ; it was, in fact,
quite the opposite, and the little Theresa was puzzled as to her duty in the matter. Pedro, however,
was not at all undecided.

" Give our bread and cake to a nasty old Moor ? "
he cried ; " I should say we will not, will we, sister ?

We need it for ourselves. Besides, what dreadful thing is it that the Holy Inquisition does to people who succor the infidel Moors ?"

Theresa shuddered. She knew too well all the stories of the horrible punishments that the Holy Office, known as the Inquisition of Spain, visited upon those who harbored Jews or aided the now degraded Moors. For so complete had been the conquest of the once proud possessors of Southern Spain, that they were usually known only by the contemptuous title of "Moriscoes," and were despised and hated by their "chivalrous" Christian conquerors.

But little Theresa de Cepeda was of so loving and generous a nature that even the plea of an outcast and despised Morisco moved her to pity. From her earliest childhood she had delighted in helpful and generous deeds. She repeatedly gave away, so we are told, all her pocket-money in charity, and any sign of trouble or distress found her ready and anxious to extend relief. There was really a good deal of the angelic in little Theresa, and even the risk of arousing the wrath of the Inquisition, the walls of whose gloomy dungeon in Avila she had so often looked upon with awe, could not withhold her from wishing to help this poor old man who was hunting for his lost son.

" Nay, brother," she said to little Pedro, " it can

be not so very great a crime to give food to a
starving man"; and much to Pedro's disgust, she
opened the wallet and emptied their little store of
provisions into the old beggar's hand.

"And wither are ye bound, little ones?" asked
this "tramp" of the long ago, as the children
watched their precious dinner disappear behind his
snowy beard.

"We are on a crusade, don Infidel," replied
Pedro, boldly. "A crusade against your armies
and castles, perhaps to capture them, and thus gain
the crown of martyrdom."

The old Moor looked at them sadly. "There is
scarce need for that, my children," he said. "My
people are but slaves; their armies and their castles
are lost; their beautiful cities are ruined, and there
is neither conquest nor martyrdom for Christian
youths and maidens to gain among them. Go
home, my little ones, and pray to Allah that you
and yours may never know so much of sorrow and
of trouble as do the poor Moriscoes of Spain this
day."

This was news to Theresa. No martyrdom to
be obtained among the Moors? Where then was
all the truth of her mother's romances,—where was
all the wisdom of her father's savage faith? She
had always supposed that the Moors were monsters
and djins, waiting with great fires and racks and

sharpest cimeters to put to horrible death all young Christians who came amongst them, and now here was one who begged for bread and pleaded for pity like any common beggar of Avila. Evidently something was wrong in the home stories.

As for little Pedro, he waxed more valiant as the danger lessened. He whetted his toy sword against the granite rocks and looked savagely at the old man.

"You have eaten all my bread, don Infidel," he said, "and now you would lie about your people and your castles. You are no beggar; you are the King of Cordova come here in this disguise to spy out the Christian's land. I know all about you from my mother's stories. So you must die. I shall send your head to our Emperor by my sister here, and when he shall ask her who has done this noble deed she will say, just as did Alvar Fanez to King Alfonso:

' My Cid Campeador, O king, it was who girded brand :
The Paynim king he hath o'ercome, the mightiest in the land.
Plenteous and sovereign is the spoil he from the Moor hath
    won ;
This portion, honored king and lord, he sendeth to your
    throne.'

"So, King of Cordova, bend down and let me cut off your head."

The "King of Cordova" made no movement of compliance to this gentle invitation, and the head-

strong Pedro, springing toward him, would have
caught him by the beard, had not his gentle sister
restrained him.

"I do believe he is no king, my Pedro," she said,
"but only, as he says, a poor Morisco beggar. Let
us rather try to help him.   He hath no castles I am
sure, and as for his armies——"

"His armies! there they come; look, sister!"
cried little Pedro, breaking into his sister's words;
"now will you believe me?" and following his gaze,
Theresa herself started as she saw dashing down
the mountain highway what looked to her unprac-
tised eye like a whole band of Moorish cavalry with
glimmering lances and streaming pennons.

Pedro faced the charge with drawn sword.
Theresa knelt on the ground with silver crucifix
upraised, expecting instant martyrdom, while the old
Moorish tramp, Abd-el-'Aman, believing discretion
to be the better part of valor, quietly dropped down
by the side of the rocky roadway, for well he under-
stood who were these latest comers.

The Moorish cavalry, which proved to be three
Spaniards on horseback, drew up before the young
crusaders.

"So, runaways, we have found you," cried one of
them, as he recognized the children. "Come,
Theresa, what means this folly? Whither are you
and Pedro bound?"

" We were even starting for a crusade against the Moor, Brother Jago," said Theresa, timidly, "but our Infidel friend here—why, where hath he gone? —says that there are neither Infidel castles nor Moorish armies now, and that therefore we may not be crusaders."

" But I know that he doth lie, Brother Jago," cried little Pedro, more valiant still when he saw to what his Moorish cavalry was reduced. " He is the King of Cordova, come here to spy out the land, and I was about to cut off his head when you did disturb us."

Big brother Jago de Cepeda and the two servants of his father's house laughed long and loudly.

" Crusaders and kings," he cried ; " why, we shall have the Cid himself here, if we do but wait long enough."

" Hush, brother," said young Pedro, confidentially, " say it not so loudly.   I did tell the Infidel that I was Ruy Diaz of Bivar, the Cid Campeador—and he did believe me."

And then the cavalry laughed louder than ever, and swooping down captured the young crusaders and set the truants before them on their uncomfortable Cordova saddles.   Then, turning around, they rode swiftly back to Avila with the runaways, while the old Moor, glad to have escaped rough handling from the Christian riders, grasped his staff and plodded on toward Avila and Valladolid.

So the expedition for martyrdom and crusade came to an ignominious end. But the pious desires of little Theresa did not. For, finding that martyrdom was out of the question, she proposed to her ever-ready brother that they should become hermits, and for days the two children worked away trying to build a hermitage near their father's house.

But the rough and heavy pieces of granite with which they sought to build their hermitage proved more than they could handle, and their knowledge of mason-work was about as imperfect as had been their familiarity with crusading and the country of the Moors. "The stones that we piled one upon another," wrote Theresa herself in later years, "immediately fell down, and so it came to pass that we found no means of accomplishing our wish."

The pluck and piety, however, that set this conscientious and sympathetic little girl to such impossible tasks were certain to blossom into something equally hard and unselfish when she grew to womanhood. And so it proved. Her much-loved but romance-reading mother died when she was twelve years old, and Theresa felt her loss keenly.

She was a very clever and ambitious girl, and with a mother's guiding hand removed she became impatient under the restraints which her stern old father, Don Alphonso, placed upon her. At sixteen she was an impetuous, worldly-minded, and very vain though very dignified young lady. Then her father, fearful as to her future, sent her to a convent, with orders that she should be kept in strict seclusion.

Such a punishment awoke all the feelings of conscientiousness and self-conviction that had so influenced her when she was a little girl, and Theresa, left to her own thoughts, first grew morbid, and then fell sick.

During her sickness she resolved to become a nun, persuaded her ever-faithful brother, Pedro, to become a friar, and when Don Alphonso, their father, refused his consent, the brother and sister, repeating the folly of their childhood, again ran away from home.

Then their father, seeing the uselessness of resistance, consented, and Theresa, at the age of twenty, entered a convent in Avila, and became a nun in what was known as the Order of the Carmelites.

The life of these nuns was strict, secluded, and silent; but the conscientious nature of Theresa found even the severities of this lonely life not sufficiently hard, and attaining to a position of influence in the order she obtained permission from the Pope in 1562 to found a new order which should be even more strict in its rules, and therefore, so she be-

lieved, more helpful. Thus was founded the Order
of Barefooted Carmelites, a body of priests and
nuns, who have in their peculiar way accomplished
very much for charity, gentleness, and self-help in
the world, and whose schools and convents have
been instituted in all parts of the earth.

Theresa de Cepeda died in 1582, greatly beloved and revered for her strict but gentle
life, her great and helpful charities, and her
sincere desire to benefit her fellow-men. After her
death, so great was the respect paid her that she
was canonized, as it is called : that is, lifted up as
an example of great goodness to the world ; and she
is to-day known and honored among devout Roman Catholics as St. Theresa of Avila.

Whatever we may think of the peculiar way in
which her life was spent; however we may regard
the story of her troubles with her conscience, her
understanding of what she deemed her duty, and
her sinking of what might have been a happy and
joyous life in the solitude and severity of a convent,
we cannot but think of her as one who wished to
do right, and who desired above all else to benefit
the world in which she lived and labored. Her
story is that of a most extraordinary and remarkable woman, who devoted her life to what she
deemed the thing demanded of her. Could we not,
all of us, profitably attempt to live in something

like a kindred spirit to that helpful and unselfish one that actuated this girl of the Spanish sierras?

" Here and there is born a Saint Theresa," says George Eliot, "foundress of nothing, whose loving heart-beats and sobs after an unattained goodness tremble off and are dispersed among hindrances, instead of centring in some long-recognizable deed."

But if a girl or boy, desiring to do right, will disregard the hindrances, and not simply sit and sob after an unattained goodness—if, instead, they will but do the duty nearest at hand manfully and well, the reward will come in something even more desirable than a "long-recognizable deed." It will come in the very self-gratification that will at last follow every act of courtesy, of friendliness, and of self-denial, and such a life will be of more real value to the world than all the deeds of all the crusaders, or than even the stern and austere charities of a Saint Theresa.

ELIZABETH OF TUDOR:

THE GIRL OF THE HERTFORD MANOR.

[*Afterward Queen Elizabeth of England; the "Good Queen Bess."*]
A.D. 1548.

THE iron-shod hoofs of the big gray courser rang sharply on the frozen ground, as, beneath the creaking boughs of the long-armed oaks, Launcelot Crue, the Lord Protector's fleetest courser-man, galloped across the Hertford fells or hills, and reined up his horse within the great gates of Hatfield manor-house.

" From the Lord Protector," he said ; and Master Avery Mitchell, the feodary,* who had been closely watching for this same courser-man for several anxious hours, took from his hands a scroll, on which was inscribed :

" *To Avery Mitchell, feodary of the Wards in Herts, at Hatfield House. From the Lord Protector,* THESE :"

And next, the courser-man, in secrecy, unscrewed one of the bullion buttons on his buff jerkin, and taking from it a scrap of paper, handed this also to the watchful feodary. Then, his mission ended, he repaired to the buttery to satisfy his lusty English appetite with a big dish of pasty, followed by ale and "wardens" (as certain hard pears, used chiefly for cooking, were called in those days), while the cautious Avery Mitchell, unrolling the scrap of paper, read :

" *In secrecy*, THESE : Under guise of mummers place a half-score good men and true in your Yule-tide maskyng. Well armed and safely conditioned. They will be there who shall command. Look for the green dragon of Wantley. On your allegiance. This from ye wit who."

Scarcely had the feodary read, re-read, and then destroyed this secret and singular missive, when the " Ho ! hollo ! " of Her Grace the Princess' outriders

---

* An old English term for the guardian of "certain wards of the state,' —young persons under guardianship of the government.

rang on the crisp December air, and there galloped
up to the broad doorway of the manor-house, a
gayly costumed train of lords and ladies, with
huntsmen and falconers and yeomen following on
behind.   Central in the group, flushed with her hard
gallop through the wintry air, a young girl of
fifteen, tall and trim in figure, sat her horse with
the easy grace of a practised and confident rider.
Her long velvet habit was deeply edged with fur,
and both kirtle and head-gear were of a rich purple
tinge, while from beneath the latter just peeped a
heavy coil of sunny, golden hair.   Her face was
fresh and fair, as should be that of any young girl
of fifteen, but its expression was rather that of high
spirits and of heedless and impetuous moods than
of simple maidenly beauty.

"Tilly-vally, my lord," she cried, dropping her
bridle-rein into the hands of a waiting groom,
"'t was my race to-day, was it not? Odds fish,
man!" she cried out sharply to the attendant groom;
"be ye easier with Roland's bridle there.   One
beast of his gentle mettle were worth a score of
clumsy varlets like to you! Well, said I not right,
my Lord Admiral; is not the race fairly mine, I
ask?" and, careless in act as in speech, she gave the
Lord Admiral's horse, as she spoke, so sharp a cut
with her riding whip as to make the big brute rear
in sudden surprise, and almost unhorse its rider,

while an unchecked laugh came from its fair tormentor.

"Good faith, Mistress," answered Sir Thomas Seymour, the Lord High Admiral, gracefully swallowing his exclamation of surprise, "your ladyship hath fairly won, and, sure, hath no call to punish both myself and my good Selim here by such unwarranted chastisement. Will your grace dismount?"

And, vaulting from his seat, he gallantly extended his hand to help the young girl from her horse; while, on the same instant, another in her train, a handsome young fellow of the girl's own age, knelt on the frozen ground and held her stirrup.

But this independent young maid would have none of their courtesies. Ignoring the outstretched hands of both the man and boy, she sprang lightly from her horse, and, as she did so, with a sly and sudden push of her dainty foot, she sent the kneeling lad sprawling backward, while her merry peal of laughter rang out as an accompaniment to his downfall.

"Without your help, my lords—without your help, so please you both," she cried. "Why, Dudley," she exclaimed, in mock surprise, as she threw a look over her shoulder at the prostrate boy, "are you there? Beshrew me, though, you do look like one of goodman Roger's Dorking cocks in the poultry yonder, so red and ruffled of feather do you seem.   There, see now, I do repent me of my discourtesy.   You, Sir Robert, shall squire me to the hall, and Lord Seymour must even content himself with playing the gallant to good Mistress Ashley " ; and, leaning on the arm of the now pacified Dudley, the self-willed girl tripped lightly up the entrance-steps.

Self-willed and thoughtless—even rude and hoydenish—we may think her in these days of gentler manners and more guarded speech.   But those were less refined and cultured times than these in which we live ; and the rough, uncurbed nature of " Kinge Henrye the viij. of Most Famous Memorye," as the old chronicles term the " bluff King Hal," reappeared to a noticeable extent in the person of his second child, the daughter of ill-fated Anne Boleyn —" my ladye's grace " the Princess Elizabeth of England.

And yet we should be readier to excuse this impetuous young princess of three hundred years ago than were even her associates and enemies.   For enemies she had, poor child, envious and vindictive ones, who sought to work her harm.   Varied and unhappy had her young life already been.   Born amid splendid hopes, in the royal palace of Greenwich ; called Elizabeth after that grandmother, the fair heiress of the House of York, whose marriage

"WITHOUT YOUR HELP, MY LORDS! WITHOUT YOUR HELP!"

to a prince of the House of Lancaster had ended
the long and cruel War or the Roses ; she had
been welcomed with the peal of bells and the boom
of cannon, and christened with all the regal ceremonial of King Henry's regal court.   Then, when
scarcely three years old, disgraced by the wicked
murder of her mother, cast off and repudiated by
her brutal father, and only received again to favor
at the christening of her baby brother, passing her
childish days in grim old castles and a wicked court,
—she found herself, at thirteen, fatherless as well
as motherless, and at fifteen cast on her own re-
sources, the sport of men's ambitions and of conspirators' schemes.   To-day the girl of fifteen,
tenderly reared, shielded from trouble by a mother's
watchful love and a father's loving care, can know
but little of the dangers that compassed this princess of England, the Lady Elizabeth.   Deliberately
separated from her younger brother, the king, by
his unwise and selfish counsellors, hated by her
elder sister, the Lady Mary, as the daughter of the
woman who had made *her* mother's life so miserable, she was, even in her manor-home of Hatfield,
where she should have been most secure, in still
greater jeopardy.   For this same Lord Seymour of
Sudleye, who was at once Lord High Admiral of
England, uncle to the king, and brother of Somerset the Lord Protector, had by fair promises and

lavish gifts bound to his purpose this defenceless girl's only protectors, Master Parry, her cofferer, or steward, and Mistress Katherine Ashley, her governess. And that purpose was to force the young princess into a marriage with himself, so as to help his schemes of treason against the Lord Protector, and get into his own hands the care of the boy king and the government of the realm. It was a bold plot, and, if unsuccessful, meant attainder and death for high treason ; but Seymour, ambitious, reckless, and unprincipled, thought only of his own desires, and cared little for the possible ruin into which he was dragging the unsuspecting and orphaned daughter of the king who had been his ready friend and patron.

So matters stood at the period of our store, on the eve of the Christmas festivities of 1548, as, on the arm of her boy escort, Sir Robert Dudley, gentleman usher at King Edward's court, and, years after, the famous Earl of Leicester of Queen Elizabeth's day, the royal maiden entered the hall of Hatfield House. And, within the great hall, she was greeted by Master Parry, her cofferer, Master Runyon, her yeoman of the robes, and Master Mitchell, the feodary. Then, with a low obeisance, the feodary presented her the scroll which had been brought him, post-haste, by Launcelot Crue, the courser-man.

"What, good Master Avery," exclaimed Elizabeth, as she ran her eye over the scroll, "you to be
Lord of Misrule and Master of the Revels! And
by my Lord of Somerset's own appointing? I am
right glad to learn it."

And this is what she read:

"*Imprimis* * : I give leave to Avery Mitchell, feodary, gentleman, to be Lord of Misrule of all good orders, at the Manor
of Hatfield, during the twelve days of Yule-tide. And, also, I
give free leave to the said Avery Mitchell to command all and
every person or persons whatsoever, as well servants as others,
to be at his command whensoever he shall sound his trumpet
or music, and to do him good service, as though I were present
myself, at their perils. I give full power and authority to his
lordship to break all locks, bolts, bars, doors, and latches to
come at all those who presume to disobey his lordship's commands. God save the King.   SOMERSET."

It was Christmas Eve. The great hall of Hatfield House gleamed with the light of many candles
that flashed upon the sconce and armor and polished
floor. Holly and mistletoe, rosemary and bay, and
all the decorations of an old-time English Christmas were tastefully arranged. A burst of laughter
ran through the hall, as through the ample doorway, and down the broad stair, trooped the motley
train of the Lord of Misrule to open the Christmas
revels. A fierce and ferocious-looking fellow was

* A Latin term signifying "in the first place," or "to commence with,'
and used as the opening of legal or official directions.

'DOWN THE BROAD STAIRS TROOPED THE MOTLEY TRAIN OF THE LORD OF MISRULE.'

he, with his great green mustache and his ogre-like
face.   His dress was a gorgeous parti-colored jerkin
and half-hose, trunks, ruff, slouch-boots of Cordova
leather, and high befeathered steeple hat.   His long
staff, topped with a fool's head, cap, and bells, rang
loudly on the floor, as, preceded by his diminutive
but pompous page, he led his train around and
around the great hall, lustily singing the chorus:

> " Like prince and king he leads the ring;
>   Right merrily we go.   Sing hey-trix, trim-go-trix,
>   Under the mistletoe ! "

A menagerie let loose, or the most dyspeptic of
after-dinner dreams, could not be more bewildering
than was this motley train of the Lord of Misrule.
Giants and dwarfs, dragons and griffins, hobby-
horses and goblins, Robin Hood and the Grand
Turk, bears and boars and fantastic animals that
never had a name, boys and girls, men and women,
in every imaginable costume and device—around
and around the hall they went, still ringing out the
chorus :

> " Sing hey-trix, trim-go-trix,
>   Under the mistletoe ! "

Then, standing in the centre of his court, the
Lord of Misrule bade his herald declare that from
Christmas Eve to Twelfth Night he was Lord Su-
preme ; that, with his magic art, he transformed all

there into children, and charged them, on their
fealty to act only as such. " I absolve them all
from wisdom," he said ; " I bid them be just wise
enough to make fools of themselves, and do decree
that none shall sit apart in pride and eke in self-
sufficiency to laugh at others " ; and then the fun
commenced.

Off in stately Whitehall, in the palace of the boy
king, her brother, the revels were grander and
showier ; but to the young Elizabeth, not yet skilled
in all the stiffness of the royal court, the Yule-tide
feast at Hatfield House brought pleasure enough ;
and so, seated at her holly-trimmed virginal—that
great-great-grandfather of the piano of to-day,—
she, whose rare skill as a musician has come
down to us, would—when wearied with her
"prankes and japes "—"tap through " some fitting
Christmas carol, or that older lay of the Yule-tide
" Mumming " :

" To shorten winter's sadness see where the folks with gladness
  Disguised, are all a-coming, right wantonly a-mumming,
                                      Fa-la !

" Whilst youthful sports are lasting, to feasting turn our fasting:
  With revels and with wassails make grief and care our vassals,
                                      Fa-la ! "

The Yule-log had been noisily dragged in " to
the firing," and as the big sparks raced up the wide
chimney, the boar's head and the tankard of sack,

the great Christmas candle and the Christmas pie,
were escorted around the room to the flourish of
trumpets and welcoming shouts ; the Lord of Misrule, with a wave of his staff, was about to give the
order for all to unmask, when suddenly there
appeared in the circle a new character—a great
green dragon, as fierce and ferocious as well could
be, from his pasteboard jaws to his curling canvas
tail. The green dragon of Wantley ! Terrified
urchins backed hastily away from his horrible jaws,
and the Lord of Misrule gave a sudden and visible
start. The dragon himself, scarce waiting for the
surprise to subside, waved his paw for silence, and
said, in a hollow, pasteboardy voice :

" Most noble Lord of Misrule, before your feast
commences and the masks are doff'd, may we not
as that which should give good appetite to all,—
with your lordship's permit and that of my lady's
grace,—tell each some wonder-filling tale as suits
the goodly time of Yule ? Here be stout maskers
can tell us strange tales of fairies and goblins, or,
perchance, of the foreign folk with whom they have
trafficked in Calicute and Affrica, Barbaria, Perew,
and other diverse lands and countries over-sea.
And after they have ended, then will I essay a
tale that shall cap them all, so past belief shall it
appear."

The close of the dragon's speech, of course, made

them all the more curious ; and the Lady Elizabeth
did but speak for all when she said : " I pray you,
good Sir Dragon, let us have your tale first. We
have had enow of Barbaria and Perew. If that
yours may be so wondrous, let us hear it even now,
and then may we decide."

" As your lady's grace wishes," said the dragon.
" But methinks when you have heard me through,
you would that it had been the last or else not told
at all."

" Your lordship of Misrule and my lady's grace
must know," began the dragon, " that my story,
though a short, is a startling one. Once on a time
there lived a king, who, though but a boy, did, by
God's grace, in talent, industry, perseverance, and
knowledge, surpass both his own years and the belief of men. And because he was good and gentle
alike and conditioned beyond the measure of his
years, he was the greater prey to the wicked wiles
of traitorous men. And one such, high in the
king's court, thought to work him ill ; and to carry
out his ends did wantonly awaken seditious and
rebellious intent even among the king's kith and
kin, whom he traitorously sought to wed,—his royal
and younger sister, — nay, start not my lady's
grace ! " exclaimed the dragon quickly, as Elizabeth
turned upon him a look of sudden and haughty
surprise. " All is known ! And this is the ending

of my wondrous tale. My Lord Seymour of Sudleye
is this day taken for high treason and haled* to the
Tower. They of your own household are held as
accomplice to the Lord Admiral's wicked intent,
and you, Lady Elizabeth Tudor, are by order of the
council to be restrained in prison wards in this
your manor of Hatfield until such time as the king's
Majesty and the honorable council shall decide.
This on your allegiance!"

The cry of terror that the dragon's words awoke,
died into silence as the Lady Elizabeth rose to her
feet, flushed with anger.

"Is this a fable or the posy of a ring, Sir
Dragon?" she said, sharply. "Do you come to
try or tempt me, or is this perchance but some part
of my Lord of Misrule's Yule-tide mumming?
'Sblood, sir; only cravens sneak behind masks to
strike and threaten. Have off your disguise, if you
be a true man; or, by my word as Princess of
England, he shall bitterly rue the day who dares to
befool the daughter of Henry Tudor!"

"As you will, then, my lady," said the dragon.
"Do you doubt me now?" and, tearing off his
pasteboard wrapping, he stood disclosed before
them all as the grim Sir Robert Trywhitt, chief ex-
aminer of the Lord Protector's council. "Move
not at your peril," he said, as a stir in the throng

* Haled—dragged, forcibly conveyed.

seemed to indicate the presence of some brave spirits who would have shielded their young princess. "Master Feodary, bid your varlets stand to their arms."

And at a word from Master Avery Mitchell, late Lord of Misrule, there flashed from beneath the cloaks of certain tall figures on the circle's edge the halberds of the guard. The surprise was complete. The Lady Elizabeth was a prisoner in her own manor-house, and the Yule-tide revels had reached a sudden and sorry ending.

And yet, once again, under this false accusation, did the hot spirit of the Tudors flame in the face and speech of the Princess Elizabeth.

"Sir Robert Trywhitt," cried the brave young girl, "these be but lying rumors that do go against my honor and my fealty. God knoweth they be shameful slanders, sir; for the which, besides the desire I have to see the King's Majesty, I pray you let me also be brought straight before the court that I may disprove these perjured tongues."

But her appeal was not granted. For months she was kept close prisoner at Hatfield House, subject daily to most rigid cross-examination by Sir Robert Trywhitt for the purpose of implicating her if possible in the Lord Admiral's plot. But all in vain; and at last even Sir Robert gave up the attempt, and wrote to the council that "the Lady

Elizabeth hath a good wit, and nothing is gotten of her but by great policy."

Lord Seymour of Sudleye, was beheaded for treason on Tower Hill, and others, implicated in his plots, were variously punished ; but even "great policy" cannot squeeze a lie out of the truth, and Elizabeth was finally declared free of the stain of treason.

Experience, which is a hard teacher, often brings to light the best that is in us. It was so in this case. For, as one writer says : "The long and harassing ordeal disclosed the splendid courage, the reticence, the rare discretion, which were to carry the Princess through many an awful peril in the years to come. Probably no event of her early girlhood went so far toward making a woman of Elizabeth as did this miserable affair."

Within ten years thereafter the Lady Elizabeth ascended the throne of England. Those ten years covered many strange events, many varying fortunes—the death of her brother, the boy King Edward, the sad tragedy of Lady Jane Grey, Wyatt's rebellion, the tanner's revolt, and all the long horror of the reign of "Bloody Mary." You may read of all this in history, and may see how, through it all, the young princess grew still more firm of will, more self-reliant, wise, and strong, developing all those peculiar qualities that helped to make her

England's greatest queen, and one of the most wonderful women in history. But through all her long and most historic life,—a life of over seventy years, forty-five of which were passed as England's queen,—scarce any incident made so lasting an impression upon her as when, in Hatfield House, the first shock of the false charge of treason fell upon the thoughtless girl of fifteen in the midst of the Christmas revels.

CHRISTINA OF SWEDEN:

THE GIRL OF THE NORTHERN FIORDS.

A.D. 1636.

THERE were tears and trouble in Stockholm; there was sorrow in every house and hamlet in Sweden; there was consternation throughout Protestant Europe. Gustavus Adolphus was dead! The "Lion of the North" had fallen on the bloody and victorious field of Lutzen, and only a very small girl of six stood as the representative of Sweden's royalty.

The States of Sweden—that is, the representatives of the different sections and peoples of the kingdom—gathered in haste within the Riddarhaus, or Hall of Assembly, in Stockholm. There was much anxious controversy over the situation. The nation was in desperate strait, and some were for one thing and some were for another. There was even talk of making the government a republic, like the state of Venice; and the supporters of the king of Poland, cousin to the dead King Gustavus, openly advocated his claim to the throne.

But the Grand Chancellor, Axel Oxenstiern, one of Sweden's greatest statesmen, acted promptly.

" Let there be no talk between us," he said, " of Venetian republics or of Polish kings. We have but one king—the daughter of the immortal Gustavus !"

Then up spoke one of the leading representatives of the peasant class, Lars Larsson, the deputy from the western fiords.

" Who is this daughter of Gustavus ? " he demanded. How do we know this is no trick of yours, Axel Oxenstiern ? How do we know that King Gustavus has a daughter ? We have never seen her."

" You shall see her at once," replied the Chancellor ; and leaving the Hall for an instant, he returned speedily, leading a little girl by the hand. With a sudden movement he lifted her to the seat of the high silver throne that could only be occupied by the kings of Sweden.

" Swedes, behold your king !"

Lars Larsson, the deputy, pressed close to the throne on which the small figure perched silent, yet with a defiant little look upon her face.

" She hath the face of the Grand Gustavus," he said. Look, brothers, the nose, the eyes, the very brows are his."

"Aye," said Oxenstiern ; "and she is a soldier's daughter.   I myself did see her, when scarce three years old, clap her tiny hands and laugh aloud when the guns of Calmar fortress thundered a salute.   'She must learn to bear it,' said Gustavus our king ; 'she is a soldier's daughter.'"

"Hail, Christina!" shouted the assembly, won by the proud bearing of the little girl and by her likeness to her valiant father.   "We will have her and only her for our queen!"

"Better yet, brothers," cried Lars Larsson, now her most loyal supporter ; "she sits upon the throne of the kings ; let her be proclaimed King of Sweden."

And so it was done.   And with their wavering loyalty kindled into a sudden flame, the States of Sweden "gave a mighty shout" and cried as one man, "Hail, Christina, King of Sweden!"

There was strong objection in Sweden to the rule of a woman ; and the education of this little girl was rather that of a prince than of a princess. She was taught to ride and to shoot, to hunt and to fence, to undertake all of a boy's exercises, and to endure all a boy's privations.   She could bring down a hare, at the first shot, from the back of a galloping horse ; she could outride the most expert huntsman in her train.

So she grew from childhood into girlhood, and

at thirteen was as bold and fearless, as wilful and self-possessed as any young fellow of twenty-one. But besides all this she was a wonderful scholar; indeed, she would be accounted remarkable even in these days of bright girl-graduates. At thirteen she was a thorough Greek scholar; she was learned in mathematics and astronomy, the classics, history, and philosophy; and she acquired of her own accord German, Italian, Spanish, and French.

Altogether, this girl Queen of the North was as strange a compound of scholar and hoyden, pride and carelessness, ambition and indifference, culture and rudeness, as ever, before her time or since, were combined in the nature of a girl of thirteen. And it is thus that our story finds her.

One raw October morning in the year 1639, there was stir and excitement at the palace in Stockholm. A courier had arrived bearing important dispatches to the Council of Regents which governed Sweden during the minority of the Queen, and there was no one to officially meet him.

Closely following the lackey who received him, the courier strode into the council-room of the palace. But the council-room was vacant.

It was not a very elegant apartment, this council-room of the palace of the kings of Sweden. Although a royal apartment, its appearance was ample proof that the art of decoration was as yet un-

known in Sweden. The room was untidy and disordered ; the council-table was strewn with the
ungathered litter of the last day's council, and
even the remains of a coarse lunch mingled with all
this clutter. The uncomfortable-looking chairs all
were out of place, and above the table was a sort
of temporary canopy to prevent the dust and
spiders' webs upon the ceiling from dropping upon
the councillors.

The courier gave a sneering look upon this
evidence that the refinement and culture which
marked at least the palaces and castles of other
European countries were as yet little considered
in Sweden. Then, important and impatient, he
turned to the attendant. " Well," he said, " and is
there none here to receive my dispatches ? They
call for—houf ! so ! what manners are these ? "

What manners indeed ! The courier might well
ask this. For, plump against him, as he spoke,
dashed, first a girl and then a boy who had darted
from somewhere into the council-chamber. Too
absorbed in their own concerns to notice who, if
any one, was in the room, they had run against and
very nearly upset the astonished bearer of dispatches. Still more astonished was he, when the
girl, using his body as a barrier against her pursuer, danced and dodged around him to avoid
being caught by her pursuer—a fine-looking young

lad of about her own age—Karl Gustav, her cousin.
The scandalized bearer of dispatches to the Swedish Council of Regents shook himself free from the
girl's strong grasp and seizing her by the shoulder,
demanded, sternly:

"How now, young mistress! Is this seemly
conduct toward a stranger and an imperial
courier?"

The girl now for the first time noticed the presence of a stranger. Too excited in her mad dash
into the room to distinguish him from one of the
palace servants, she only learned the truth by the
courier's harsh words. A sudden change came
over her. She drew herself up haughtily and said
to the attendant:

"And who is this officious stranger, Klas?"

The tone and manner of the question again surprised the courier, and he looked at the speaker,
amazed. What he saw was an attractive young
girl of thirteen, short of stature, with bright hazel
eyes, a vivacious face, now almost stern in its expression of pride and haughtiness. A man's fur
cap rested upon the mass of tangled light-brown
hair which, tied imperfectly with a simple knot of
ribbon, fell down upon her neck. Her short dress
of plain gray stuff hung loosely about a rather trim
figure; and a black scarf, carelessly tied, encircled
her neck. In short, he saw a rather pretty, care

lessly dressed, healthy, and just now very haughty-
looking young girl, who seemed more like a boy in
speech and manners,—and one who needed to be
disciplined and curbed.

Again the question came: "Who is this man,
and what seeks he here, Klas? I ask."

"'T is a courier with dispatches for the council,
Madam," replied the man.

"Give me the dispatches," said the girl; "I will
attend to them."

"You, indeed!" The courier laughed grimly.
"The dispatches from the Emperor of Germany
are for no hairbrained maid to handle. These are
to be delivered to the Council of Regents alone."

"I will have naught of councils or regents,
Sir Courier, save when it pleases me," said the
girl, tapping the floor with an angry foot. "Give
me the dispatches, I say,—I am the King of
Sweden!"

"You—a girl—king?" was all that the astonished courier could stammer out. Then, as the real
facts dawned upon him, he knelt at the feet of the
young queen and presented his dispatches.

"Withdraw, sir!" said Christina, taking the
papers from his hand with but the scant courtesy
of a nod; "we will read these and return a suitable answer to your master."

The courier withdrew, still dazed at this strange

"I AM THE KING OF SWEDEN," SAID CHRISTINA.

turn of affairs; and Christina, leaning carelessly against the council-table, opened the dispatches.

Suddenly she burst into a merry but scarcely lady-like laugh. "Ha, ha, ha! this is too rare a joke, Karl," she cried. "Lord Chancellor, Mathias, Torstenson!" she exclaimed, as these members of her council entered the apartment, "what think you? Here come dispatches from the Emperor of Germany begging that you, my council, shall consider the wisdom of wedding me to his son and thereby closing the war! His son, indeed! Ferdinand the Craven!"

"And yet, Madam," suggested the wise Oxenstiern, "it is a matter that should not lightly be cast aside. In time you must needs be married. The constitution of the kingdom doth oblige you to."

"Oblige!" and the young girl turned upon the gray-headed chancellor almost savagely. "Oblige! and who, Sir Chancellor, upon earth shall *oblige* me to do so, if I do it not of mine own will? Say not *oblige* to me."

This was vigorous language for a girl of scarce fourteen; but it was "Christina's way," one with which both the Council and the people soon grew familiar. It was the Vasa* nature in her, and it

---

* Vasa was the family name of her father and the ancient king of Sweder

was always prominent in this spirited young girl—
the last descendant of that masterful house.

But now the young Prince Karl Gustavus had
something to say.

"Ah, cousin mine," and he laid a strong though
boyish hand upon the young girl's arm. "What
need for couriers or dispatches that speak of suitors
for your hand? Am not I to be your husband?
From babyhood you have so promised me."

Christina again broke into a loud and merry
laugh.

"Hark to the little burgomaster," * she cried;
"much travel hath made him, I do fear me, soft in
heart and head. Childish promises, Karl. Let
such things be forgotten now. You are to be a
soldier—I, a queen."

"And yet, Madam," said Mathias, her tutor, "all
Europe hath for years regarded Prince Karl as your
future husband."

"And what care I for that?" demanded the girl,
hotly. "Have done, have done, sirs! You do
weary me with all this. Let us to the hunt. Axel
Dagg did tell me of a fine roebuck in the Maelar
woods. See you to the courier of the Emperor and

---

* Prince Charles Gustavus, afterward Charles XI., King of Sweden, and
father of the famous Charles XII., was cousin to Christina. He was short
and thick-set, and so like a little Dutchman that Christina often called him
"the little burgomaster." At the time of this sketch he had just returned
from a year of travel through Europe.

to his dispatches, Lord Chancellor ; I care not what you tell him, if you do but tell him no. And, stay ; where is that round little Dutchman, Van Beunigen, whom you did complain but yesterday was sent among us by his government to oppose the advices of our English friends. He is a greater scholar than horseman, or I mistake. Let us take him in our hunting-party, Karl ; and see to it that he doth have one of our choicest horses."

The girl's mischief was catching. Her cousin dropped his serious look, and, seeking the Dutch envoy, with due courtesy invited him to join the Queen's hunt.

" Give him black Hannibal, Joüs," Christina had said to her groom ; and when the Dutch envoy, Van Beunigen, came out to join the hunting-party, too much flattered by the invitation to remember that he was a poor horseman, Joüs, the groom, held black Hannibal in unsteady check, while the big horse champed and fretted, and the hunting-party awaited the new member.

But Joüs, the groom, noted the Dutchman's somewhat alarmed look at the big black animal.

" Would it not be well, good sir," he said, "that you do choose some steadier animal than Hannibal here ?   I pray you let me give you one less restive. So, Bror Andersson," he called to one of the under-grooms, "let the noble envoy have your cob, and take you back Hannibal to the stables."

But no, the envoy of the States of Holland would submit to no such change. He ride a servant's horse, indeed !

" Why, sirrah groom," he said to good-hearted Joüs, " I would have you know that I am no novice in the equestrian art. Far from it, man. I have read every treatise on the subject from Xenophon downward ; and what horse can know more than I ? "

So friendly Joüs had nothing more to say, but hoisted the puffed-up Dutch scholar into the high saddle ; and away galloped the hunt toward the Maelar woods.

As if blind to his own folly, Van Beunigen, the envoy, placed himself near to the young Queen ; and Christina, full of her own mischief, began gravely to compliment him on his horsemanship, and suggested a gallop.

Alas, fatal moment. For while he yet swayed and jolted upon the back of the restive Hannibal, and even endeavored to discuss with the fair young scholar who rode beside him, the " Melanippe " of Euripides, the same fair scholar—who, in spite of all her Greek learning was only a mischievous and sometimes very rude young girl—faced him with a sober countenance.

" Good Herr Van Beunigen," she said, " your Greek is truly as smooth as your face. But it seems to me you do not sufficiently catch the spirit of the poet's lines commmencing ἀνδρῶν δὲ πολλοὶ τοῦ γέλωτος οὕνεκα.*

I should rather say that τοῦ γέλωτος should be———"

Just what τοῦ γέλωτος should be she never declared, for, as the envoy of Holland turned upon her a face on which Greek learning and anxious horsemanship struggled with one another, Christina slyly touched black Hannibal lightly with her riding-whip.

Light as the touch was, however, it was enough. The unruly horse reared and plunged. The startled scholar, with a cry of terror, flung up his hands, and then clutched black Hannibal around the neck. Thus, in the manner of John Gilpin,

> " His horse, who never in that way
> Had handled been before,
> What thing upon his back had got
> Did wonder more and more.

> "Away went Gilpin, neck or nought ;
> Away went hat and wig ;
> He never dreamt when he set out,
> Of running such a rig."

Minus hat and wig, too, the poor envoy dashed up the Maelar highway, while Christina, laughing loudly, galloped after him in a mad race, followed by all her hunting-party.

The catastrophe was not far away. The black

---

* The commencement of an extract from the "Melanippe" of Euripides, meaning, "To raise vain laughter, many exercise the arts of satire."

"MINUS HAT AND WIG THE POOR ENVOY DASHED UP THE MAELAR HIGHWAY."

horse, like the ill-tempered "bronchos" of our western plains, "bucked" suddenly, and over his head like a flash went the discomfited Dutchman. In an instant, Greek learning and Dutch diplomacy lay sprawling in a Swedish roadway, from which Joüs, the groom, speedily lifted the groaning would-be horseman.

Even in her zeal for study, really remarkable in so young a girl, Christina could not forego her misguided love of power and her tendency to practical joking, and one day she even made two grave philosophers, who were holding a profound discussion in her presence over some deep philosophic subject, suddenly cease their arguments to play with her at battledore and shuttlecock.

A girlhood of uncontrolled power, such as hers, could lead but to one result. Self-gratification is the worst form of selfishness, and never can work good to any one. Although she was a girl of wonderful capabilities, of the blood of famous kings and conquerors, giving such promises of greatness that scholars and statesmen alike prophesied for her a splendid future, Christina, Queen of Sweden, made only a failure of her life.

At eighteen she had herself formally crowned as *King* of Sweden. But at twenty-five she declared herself sick and tired of her duties as queen, and at twenty-eight, at the height of her power and fame, she actually did resign her throne in favor of her cousin, Prince Karl,—publicly abdicated, and at once left her native land to lead the life of a disappointed wanderer.

The story of this remarkable woman is one that holds a lesson for all. Eccentric, careless, and fearless; handsome, witty, and learned; ambitious, shrewd, and visionary,—she was one of the strangest compounds of "unlikes" to be met with in history.

She deliberately threw away a crown, wasted a life that might have been helpful to her subjects, regarded only her own selfish and personal desires, and died a prematurely old woman at sixty-five, unloved and unhonored.

Her story, if it teaches any thing, assures us that it is always best to have in youth, whether as girl or boy, the guidance and direction of some will that is acknowledged and respected. Natures unformed or over-indulged, with none to counsel or command, generally go wrong. A mother's love, a father's care, these—though young people may not always read them aright—are needed for the moulding of character; while to every bright young girl, historic or unhistoric, princess or peasant, Swedish queen or modern American maiden, will it at last be apparent that the right way is always the way of modesty and gentleness, of high ambitions, perhaps, but, always and everywhere, of thoughtfulness for others and kindliness to all.

MA-TA-OKA OF POW-HA-TAN:

THE GIRL OF THE VIRGINIA FORESTS.

[Generally known as "The Princess Pocahontas."]
A.D. 1607.

THROUGHOUT that portion of the easterly United States where the noble bay called the Chesapeake cuts Virginia in two, and where the James, broadest of all the rivers of the "Old Dominion," rolls its glittering waters toward the sea, there lived, years ago, a notable race of men.

For generations they had held the land, and, though their clothing was scanty and their customs odd, they possessed many of the elements of character that are esteemed noble, and, had they been left to themselves, they might have progressed—so people who have studied into their character now believe—into a fairly advanced stage of what is known as barbaric civilization.

They lived in long, low houses of bark and boughs, each house large enough to accommodate, perhaps, from eighty to a hundred persons—twenty families to a house. These "long houses" were, therefore, much the same in purpose as are the tenement-houses of to-day, save that the tenements of that far-off time were all on the same floor and were open closets or stalls, about eight feet wide, furnished with bunks built against the wall and spread with deer-skin robes for comfort and covering. These "flats" or stalls were arranged on either side of a broad, central passage-way, and in this passage-way, at equal distances apart, fire pits were constructed, the heat from which would warm the bodies and cook the dinners of the occupants of the "long house," each fire serving the purpose of four tenements or families.

In their mode of life these people—tall, well-made, attractive, and coppery-colored folk—were what is now termed communists, that is, they lived from common stores and had all an equal share in the land and its yield—the products of their vegetable gardens, their hunting and fishing expeditions, their home labors, and their household goods.

Their method of government was entirely democratic. No one, in any household, was better off or of higher rank than his brothers or sisters. Their chiefs were simply men (and sometimes women) who had been raised to leadership by the desire and vote of their associates, but who possessed no special authority or power, except such as was al-

lowed them by the general consent of their comrades, in view of their wisdom, bravery, or ability.
They lived, in fact, as one great family bound in
close association by their habits of life and their
family relationships, and they knew no such un-
natural distinction as king or subject, lord or vassal.

Around their long bark tenements, stretched care-
fully cultivated fields of corn and pumpkins, the
trailing bean, the full-bunched grapevine, the juicy
melon, and the big-leafed *tabah*, or tobacco.

The field work was performed by the women, not
from any necessity of a slavish condition or an en-
forced obedience, but because, where the men and
boys must be warriors and hunters, the women and
girls felt that it was their place and their duty to
perform such menial labor as, to their unenlightened
nature, seemed hardly suitable to those who were
to become chiefs and heroes.

These sturdy forest-folk of old Virginia, who
had reached that state of human advance, midway between savagery and civilization, that is
known as barbarism, were but a small portion of
that red-skinned, vigorous, and most interesting
race familiar to us under their general but wrongly-
used name of " Indians." They belonged to one of
the largest divisions of this barbaric race, known as
the Algonquin family—a division created solely by
a similarity of language and of blood-relationships

—and were, therefore, of the kindred of the Indians of Canada, of New England, and of Pennsylvania, of the valley of the Ohio, the island of Manhattan, and of some of the far-away lands beyond the Mississippi.

So, for generations, they lived, with their simple home customs and their family affections, with their games and sports, their legends and their songs, their dances, fasts, and feasts, their hunting and their fishing, their tribal feuds and wars. They had but little religious belief, save that founded upon the superstition that lies at the foundation of all uncivilized intelligence, and though their customs show a certain strain of cruelty in their nature, this was not a savage and vindictive cruelty, but was, rather, the result of what was, from their way of looking at things, an entirely justifiable understanding of order and of law.

At the time of our story, certain of these Algonquin tribes of Virginia were joined together in a sort of Indian republic, composed of thirty tribes scattered through Central and Eastern Virginia, and known to their neighbors as the Confederacy of the Pow-ha-tans. This name was taken from the tribe that was at once the strongest and the most energetic one in this tribal union, and that had its fields and villages along the broad river known to the Indians as the Pow-ha-tan, and to us as the James.

The principal chief of the Pow-ha-tans was Wa-bun-so-na-cook, called by the white men Pow-ha-tan. He was a strongly built but rather stern-faced old gentleman of about sixty, and possessed such an influence over his tribesmen that he was regarded as the head man (president, we might say), of their forest republic, which comprised the thirty confederated tribes of Pow-ha-tan. The confederacy, in its strongest days, never numbered more than eight or nine thousand people, and yet it was considered one of the largest Indian unions in America. This, therefore, may be considered as pretty good proof that there was never, after all, a very extensive Indian population in America, even before the white man discovered it.

Into one of the Pow-ha-tan villages that stood very near the shores of Chesapeake Bay, and almost opposite the now historic site of Yorktown, came one biting day, in the winter of 1607, an Indian runner, whose name was Ra-bun-ta. He came as one that had important news to tell, but he paused not for shout or question from the inquisitive boys who were tumbling about in the light snow, in their favorite sport of *Ga-wá-sa* or the "snow-snake" game. One of the boys, a mischievous and sturdy young Indian of thirteen, whose name was Nan-ta-qua-us, even tried to insert the slender knob-headed stick, which was the "snake" in

the game, between the runner's legs, and trip him
up. But Ra-bun-ta was too skilful a runner to be
stopped by trifles; he simply kicked the "snake"
out of his way, and hurried on to the long house of
the chief.

Now this Indian settlement into which the runner had come was the Pow-ha-tan village of Wero-
woco-moco, and was the one in which the old chief
Wa-bun-so-na-cook usually resided. Here was the
long council-house in which the chieftains of the
various tribes in the confederacy met for counsel
and for action, and here, too, was the "long tene-
ment-house" in which the old chief and his immediate family lived.

It was into this dwelling that the runner dashed.
In a group about the central fire-pit he saw the
chief. Even before he could himself stop his headlong speed, however, his race with news came to
an unexpected end. The five fires were all surrounded by lolling Indians, for the weather in that
winter of 1607 was terribly cold, and an Indian,
when inside his house, always likes to get as near
to the fire as possible. But down the long passage-
way the children were noisily playing at their
games—at *gus-kä-eh*, or "peach-pits," at *gus-ga-e-
sá-tä*, or "deer-buttons," and some of the younger
boys were turning wonderful somersaults up and
down the open spaces between the fire-pits. Just

as the runner, Ra-bun-ta, sped up the passage-way, one of these youthful gymnasts with a dizzy succession of hand-springs came whizzing down the passage-way right in the path of Ra-bun-ta.

There was a sudden collision. The tumbler's stout little feet came plump against the breast of Ra-bun-ta, and so sudden and unexpected was the shock that both recoiled, and runner and gymnast alike tumbled over in a writhing heap upon the very edge of one of the big bonfires. Then there was a great shout of laughter, for the Indians dearly loved a joke, and such a rough piece of unintentional pleasantry was especially relished.

" Wà, wà, Ra-bun-ta," they shouted, pointing at the discomfited runner as he picked himself out of the fire, " knocked over by a girl ! "

And the deep voice of the old chief said half sternly, half tenderly :

" My daughter, you have wellnigh killed our brother Ra-bun-ta with your foolery. That is scarce girls' play. Why will you be such a *po-ca-hun-tas ?* " *

The runner joined in the laugh against him quite as merrily as did the rest, and made a dash at the little ten-year-old tumbler, which she as nimbly evaded.

" *Ma-ma-no-to-wic,*"† he said, " the feet of Ma-ta-

---

* *Po-ca-hun-tas*, Algonquin for a little " tomboy."

† " Great man " or "strong one," a title by which Wa-bun-so-na-cook, or Powhatan, was frequently addressed.

oka are even heavier than the snake of Nun-ta-qua-
us, her brother. I have but escaped them both
with my life. *Ma-ma-no-to-wic*, I have news for
you. The braves, with your brother O-pe-chan-ca-
nough, have taken the pale-face chief in the Chicka-
hominy swamps and are bringing him to the council-house."

"Wà," said the old chief, "it is well, we will be
ready for him."

At once Ra-bun-ta was surrounded and plied
with questions. The earlier American Indians
were always a very inquisitive folk, and were great
gossips. Ra-bun-ta's news would furnish fire-pit
talk for months, so they must know all the particu-
lars. What was this white *cau-co-rouse*, (captain
or leader) like? What had he on? Did he use
his magic against the braves? Were any of them
killed?

For the fame of "the white *cau-co-rouse*," the
"great captain," as the Indians called the courageous and intrepid little governor of the Virginia
colony, Captain John Smith, had already gone
throughout the confederacy, and his capture was
even better than a victory over their deadliest enemies, the Manna-ho-acks.

Ra-bun-ta was as good a gossip and story-teller
as any of his tribesmen, and as he squatted before
the upper fire-pit, and ate a hearty meal of parched

corn, which the little Ma-ta-oka brought him as a peace-offering, he gave the details of the celebrated capture. "The 'great captain,'" he said, "and two of his men had been surprised in the Chicka-hom-iny swamps by the chief O-pe-chan-ca-nough and two hundred braves. The two men were killed by the chief, but the 'captain,' seeing himself thus en-trapped, seized his Indian guide and fastened him before as a shield, and thus sent out so much of his magic thunder from his fire-tube that he killed or wounded many of the Indians, and yet kept him-self from harm though his clothes were torn with arrow-shots. At last, however," said the runner, "the 'captain' had slipped into a mud-hole in the swamps, and, being there surrounded, was dragged out and made captive, and he, Ra-bun-ta, had been sent on to tell the great news to the chief.

The Indians especially admired bravery and cun-ning. This device of the white chieftain and his valor when attacked appealed to their admiration, and there was great desire to see him when next day he was brought into the village by the chief of the Pa-mun-kee, or York River Indians, O-pe-chan-ca-nough, brother of the chief of the Pow-ha-tans.

The renowned prisoner was received with the customary chorus of Indian yells, and then, acting upon the one leading Indian custom, the law of unlimited hospitality, a bountiful feast was set before the captive, who, like the valiant man he was, ate heartily though ignorant what his fate might be.

The Indians seldom wantonly killed their captives. When a sufficient number had been sacrificed to avenge the memory of such braves as had fallen in fight, the remaining captives were either adopted as tribesmen or disposed of as slaves.

So valiant a warrior as this pale-faced *cau-co-rouse* was too important a personage to be used as a slave, and Wa-bun-so-na-cook, the chief, received him as an honored guest* rather than as a prisoner, kept him in his own house for two days, and adopting him as his own son, promised him a large gift of land. Then, with many expressions of friendship, he returned him, well escorted by Indian guides, to the trail that led back direct to the English colony at Jamestown.

This rather destroys the long-familiar romance of the doughty captain's life being saved by "the king's own daughter," but it seems to be the only true version of the story, based upon his own original report.

But though the oft-described "rescue" did not take place, the valiant Englishman's attention was

---

* "Hee kindly welcomed me with good wordes," says Smith's own narrative, "assuring me his friendship and my libertie."

speedily drawn to the agile little Indian girl, Ma-ta-oka, whom her father called his "tomboy," or *po-ca-hun-tas.*

She was as inquisitive as any young girl, savage or civilized, and she was so full of kindly attentions to the captain, and bestowed on him so many smiles and looks of wondering curiosity, that Smith made much of her in return, gave her some trifling presents and asked her name.

Now it was one of the many singular customs of the American Indians never to tell their own names, nor even to allow them to be spoken to strangers by any of their own immediate kindred. The reason for this lay in the superstition which held that the speaking of one's real name gave to the stranger to whom it was spoken a magical and harmful influence over such person. For the Indian religion was full of what is called the supernatural.

So, when the old chief of the Pow-ha-tans (who, for this very reason, was known to the colonists by the name of his tribe, Pow-ha-tan, rather than by his real name of Wa-bun-so-na-cook) was asked his little daughter's name, he hesitated, and then gave in reply the nick-name by which he often called her, Po-ca-hun-tas, the "little tomboy"—for this agile young maiden, by reason of her relationship to the head chief, was allowed much more free-

dom and fun than was usually the lot of Indian
girls, who were, as a rule, the patient and uncom-
plaining little drudges of every Indian home and
village.

So, when Captain Smith left Wero-woco-moco,
he left one firm friend behind him,—the pretty little
Indian girl, Ma-ta-oka,—who long remembered the
white man and his presents, and determined, after
her own wilful fashion, to go into the white man's
village and see all their wonders for herself.

In less than a year she saw the captain again,
For when, in the fall of 1608, he came to her
father's village to invite the old chief to Jamestown
to be crowned by the English as "king" of the
Pow-ha-tans, this bright little girl of twelve gathered together the other little girls of the village,
and, almost upon the very spot where, many years
after, Cornwallis was to surrender the armies of
England to the "rebel" republic, she with her
companions entertained the English captain with a
gay Indian dance full of noise and frolic.

Soon after this second interview, Ma-ta-oka's wish
to see the white man's village was gratified. For
in that same autumn of 1608 she came with Ra-bun-
ta to Jamestown. She sought out the captain who
was then "president" of the colony, and "entreated
the libertie" of certain of her tribesmen who had
been "detained,"—in other words, treacherously

made prisoners by the settlers because of some fear of an Indian plot against them.

Smith was a shrewd enough man to know when to bluster and when to be friendly. He released the Indian captives at Ma-ta-oka's wish—well knowing that the little girl had been duly " coached " by her wily old father, but feeling that even the friendship of a child may often be of value to people in a strange land.

The result of this visit to Jamestown was the frequent presence in the town of the chieftain's daughter. She would come, sometimes, with her brother, Nan-ta-qua-us, sometimes with the runner, Ra-bun-ta, and sometimes with certain of her girl followers. For even little Indian girls had their " dearest friends," quite as much as have our own clannish young school-girls of to-day.

I am afraid, however, that this twelve-year-old, Ma-ta-oka, fully deserved, even when she should have been on her good behavior among the white people, the nickname of " little tomboy " (*po-ca-hun-tas*) that her father had given her,—for we have the assurance of sedate Master William Strachey, secretary of the colony, that " the before remembered Pocahontas, Powhatan's daughter, sometimes resorting to our fort, of the age then of eleven or twelve years, did get the boyes forth with her into the market-place, and make them wheele, falling on

their hands, turning their heeles upward, whome
she would followe and wheele so herself, all the fort
over." From which it would appear that she could
easily "stunt" the English boys at "making cart-
wheels."

But there came a time very soon when she came
into Jamestown for other purpose than turning
somersaults.

The Indians soon learned to distrust the white
men, because of the unfriendly and selfish dealings,
of the new-comers, their tyranny, their haughty disregard of the Indians' wishes and desires, and their
impudent meddling alike with chieftains and with
tribesmen. Discontent grew into hatred and, led
on by certain traitors in the colony, a plot was arranged for the murder of Captain Smith and the
destruction of the colony.

Three times they attempted to entrap and de-
stroy the "great captain" and his people, but each
time the little Ma-ta-oka, full of friendship and
pity for her new acquaintances, stole cautiously
into the town, or found some means of misleading
the conspirators, and thus warned her white friends
of their danger.

One dark winter night in January, 1609, Captain
Smith, who had came to Wero-woco-moco for conference and treaty with Wa-bun-so-na-cook (whom
he always called Pow-ha-tan), sat in the York River

woods awaiting some provisions that the chief had promised him,—for eatables were scarce that winter in the Virginia colony.

There was a light step beneath which the dry twigs on the ground crackled slightly, and the wary captain grasped his matchlock and bade his men be on their guard. Again the twigs crackled, and now there came from the shadow of the woods not a train of Indians, but one little girl—Ma-ta-oka, or Pocahontas.

"Be guarded, my father," she said, as Smith drew her to his side. "The corn and the good cheer will come as promised, but even now, my father, the chief of the Pow-ha-tans is gathering all his power to fall upon you and kill you. If you would live, get you away at once."

The captain prepared to act upon her advice without delay, but he felt so grateful at this latest and most hazardous proof of the little Indian girl's regard that he desired to manifest his thankfulness by presents—the surest way to reach an Indian's heart.

"My daughter," he said kindly, "you have again saved my life, coming alone, and at risk of your own young life, through the irksome woods and in this gloomy night to admonish me. Take this, I pray you, from me, and let it always tell you of the love of Captain Smith."

And the grateful pioneer handed her his much-prized pocket compass—an instrument regarded with awe by the Indians, and esteemed as one of the instruments of the white man's magic.

But Ma-ta-oka, although she longed to possess this wonderful "path-teller," shook her head.

"Not so, Cau-co-rouse," she said, "if it should be seen by my tribesmen, or even by my father, the chief, I should but be as dead to them, for they would know that I have warned you whom they have sworn to kill, and so would they kill me also. Stay not to parley, my father, but be gone at once."

And with that, says the record, "she ran away by herself as she came."

So the captain hurried back to Jamestown, and Ma-ta-oka returned to her people.

Soon after Smith left the colony, sick and worn out by the continual worries and disputes with his fellow-colonists, and Ma-ta-oka felt that, in the absence of her best friend and the increasing troubles between her tribesmen and the pale-faces, it would be unwise for her to visit Jamestown.

Her fears seem to have been well grounded, for in the spring of 1613, Ma-ta-oka, being then about sixteen, was treacherously and "by stratagem" kidnapped by the bold and unscrupulous Captain Argall—half pirate, half trader,—and was held by the colonists as hostage for the "friendship" of Pow-ha-tan.

Within these three years, however, she had been married to the chief of one of the tributary tribes, Ko-ko-um by name, but, as was the Indian marriage custom, Ko-ko-um had come to live among the kindred of his wife, and had shortly after been killed in one of the numerous Indian fights.

It was during the captivity of the young widow at Jamestown that she became acquainted with Master John Rolfe, an industrious young Englishman, and the man who, first of all the American colonists, attempted the cultivation of tobacco.

Master Rolfe was a widower and an ardent desirer of "the conversion of the pagan salvages." He became interested in the young Indian widow, and though he protests that he married her for the purpose of converting her to Christianity, and rather ungallantly calls her "an unbelieving creature," it is just possible that if she had not been a pretty and altogether captivating young unbeliever he would have found less personal means for her conversion.

Well, the Englishman and the Indian girl, as we all know, were married, lived happily together, and finally departed for England. Here, all too soon, in 1617, when she was about twenty-one, the daughter of the great chieftain of the Pow-ha-tans died.

Her story is both a pleasant and a sad one. It needs none of the additional romance that has been thrown about it to render it more interesting. An Indian girl, free as her native forests, made friends with the race that, all unnecessarily, became hostile to her own. Brighter, perhaps, than most of the girls of her tribe, she recognized and desired to avail herself of the refinements of civilization, and so gave up her barbaric surroundings, cast in her lot with the white race, and sought to make peace and friendship between neighbors take the place of quarrel and of war.

The white race has nothing to be proud of in its conquest of the people who once owned and occupied the vast area of the North American continent. The story is neither an agreeable nor a chivalrous one. But out of the gloom which surrounds it, there come some figures that relieve the darkness, the treachery, and the crime that make it so sad. And not the least impressive of these is this bright and gentle little daughter of Wa-bun-so-na-cook, chief of the Pow-ha-tans, Ma-ta-oka, friend of the white strangers, whom we of this later day know by the nickname her loving old father gave her—Po-ca-hun-tas, the Algonquin.

THE END.